Illustrated Catalogue Of The Remarkable Collection Of The Imperial Prince Kung Of China: A Wonderful Treasury Of Celestial Art Recently Acquired By The Widely Known Firm Of Yamanaka & Company, New York, Europe, China And Japan And To Be Sold At...

Yamanaka & Company, Kung Ching Wang (Prince.)

The Prince Kung Collection

AMERICAN ART GALLERIES
MADISON SQUARE SOUTH
NEW YORK

ON FREE VIEW

AT THE AMERICAN ART GALLERIES

MADISON SQUARE SOUTH, NEW YORK

BEGINNING SATURDAY, FEBRUARY 22ND, 1913

AND CONTINUING UNTIL THE DATE OF SALE

THE REMARKABLE COLLECTION

OF THE

IMPERIAL PRINCE KUNG

OF CHINA

TO BE SOLD AT UNRESTRICTED PUBLIC SALE

ON THURSDAY, FRIDAY AND SATURDAY AFTERNOONS

FEBRUARY 27TH AND 28TH AND MARCH 1ST

BEGINNING AT 2.30 O'CLOCK

AT THE AMERICAN ART GALLERIES

MADISON SQUARE SOUTH, NEW YORK

IMPERIAL PRINCE KUNG

ILLUSTRATED CATALOGUE

OF

THE REMARKABLE COLLECTION

OF THE

IMPERIAL PRINCE KUNG

OF CHINA

A WONDERFUL TREASURY OF
CELESTIAL ART

RECENTLY ACQUIRED BY THE WIDELY KNOWN FIRM OF
YAMANAKA & COMPANY
NEW YORK, EUROPE, CHINA AND JAPAN

AND

TO BE SOLD AT UNRESTRICTED PUBLIC SALE
BY THEIR ORDER

ON THE DATES HEREIN STATED

THE SALE WILL BE CONDUCTED BY
MR. THOMAS E. KIRBY, OF
THE AMERICAN ART ASSOCIATION, MANAGERS
NEW YORK
1913

CONDITIONS OF SALE

1. *The highest bidder to be the Buyer, and if any dispute arises between two or more Bidders, the Lot so in dispute shall be immediately put up again and re-sold.*

2. *The Auctioneer reserves the right to reject any bid which is merely a nominal or fractional advance, and therefore, in his judgment, likely to affect the Sale injuriously.*

3. *The Purchasers to give their names and addresses, and to pay down a cash deposit, or the whole of the Purchase-money, if required, in default of which the Lot or Lots so purchased to be immediately put up again and re-sold.*

4. *The Lots to be taken away at the Buyer's Expense and Risk* within twenty-four hours from the conclusion of the Sale, unless otherwise specified by the Auctioneer or Managers previous to or at the time of Sale, *and the remainder of the Purchase-money to be absolutely paid, or otherwise settled for to the satisfaction of the Auctioneer, on or before delivery; in default of which the undersigned will not hold themselves responsible if the lots be lost, stolen, damaged, or destroyed, but they will be left at the sole risk of the purchaser.*

5. While the undersigned will not hold themselves responsible for the correctness of the description, genuineness, or authenticity of, or any fault or defect in, any Lot, and make no Warranty whatever, they will, upon receiving previous to date of Sale trustworthy expert opinion in writing that any Painting or other Work of Art is not what it is represented to be, use every effort on their part to furnish proof to the contrary; failing in which, the object or objects in question will be sold subject to the declaration of the aforesaid expert, he being liable to the Owner or Owners thereof for damage or injury occasioned thereby.

6. *To prevent inaccuracy in delivery and inconvenience in the settlement of the Purchases, no Lot can, on any account, be removed during the Sale.*

7. *Upon failure to comply with the above conditions, the money deposited in part payment shall be forfeited; all Lots uncleared within one day from conclusion of Sale (unless otherwise specified as above) shall be re-sold by public or private sale, without further notice, and the deficiency (if any) attending such re-sale shall be made good by the defaulter at this Sale, together with all charges attending the same. This Condition is without prejudice to the right of the Auctioneer to enforce the contract made at this Sale, without such re-sale, if he thinks fit.*

8. *The Undersigned are in no manner connected with the business of the cartage or packing and shipping of purchases, and although they will afford to purchasers every facility for employing careful carriers and packers, they will not hold themselves responsible for the acts and charges of the parties engaged for such services.*

THE AMERICAN ART ASSOCIATION, MANAGERS.
THOMAS E. KIRBY, AUCTIONEER.

PREFATORY

PRINCE KUNG CHING WANG is an Imperial prince of the Manchu Dynasty, which has recently been dethroned after having ruled the Empire since the year 1644, and he had strong claims to the throne in place of the late unhappy Emperor Kuang-Sü, as the scion of an elder branch; but he did not contest Kuang-Sü's accession. Prince Kung was studious from childhood, and early showed an aptitude for foreign affairs and international relations, and his liberality was not pleasing to the reactionaries in the Government of the ancient monarchy.

He is the grandson of the first Prince Kung, who was the sixth son of the Emperor Taou-Kuang (1821-1850). The late Emperor Kuang-Sü was the grandson of the first Prince Chun, who was the seventh son of Taou-Kuang.

Taou-Kuang was succeeded by his fourth son, Hsien Fêng (1851-1861), who was succeeded by his son T'ung Chih (1862-1874) and his nephew Kuang-Sü (1875-1911). Just there was the hitch, T'ung Chih and Kuang-Sü being cousins of the same generation, and an established custom in China requiring that the one succeeding to the throne shall not be of the same generation as the latest decedent. So, the proceeding being unusual and extraordinary, there was strong reason in Prince Kung's claims to the throne at the time it passed to the younger line.

Latterly, Prince Kung's advocacy of the imminent necessity of a drastic political reformation within the Empire, an advocacy based upon his knowledge of international affairs, of course was not pleasing to the conservative elements, and the Prince removed with some precipitation from his palace to a home in the German protectorate in China, where he now dwells.

His spacious Pekin mansion is at the northwest of the Imperial Palace, surrounded by a lofty, solid wall, with a group of tall, aged and imposing trees within, and presents an impressive spectacle. It was sealed from the time of his departure until the visit of the purchasers of his art collection last summer, and there was great formality in procuring entrance. In the great dining-room everything remained, by his orders, precisely as when he left, even to a half-smoked cigarette.

Passing through one gate after another of this Imperial abode of Prince Kung, the visitor finds a straight row of buildings accommodating from three to four hundred of the Prince's followers, and the quarters of the household force. In a central location is a great building in the form of a temple pavilion, the reception-room for distinguished visitors. One passes along the veranda to the left to the great dining saloon, and across a central garden toward the right is the small library, with exhibition rooms.

In the rear section of this building, across the center of the garden, is the great library, where, besides the numerous books to left and right, mainly bronzes and jades were shown. Leaving this library at a short distance, one came to a large, solid-looking two-story building in the form of a letter L, which might be called the Fine Arts Museum, containing a countless number of precious treasures.

Through the treasure house, and by way of a stone arch, one entered a garden filled with trees and flowers of foreign lands, around the Tea House, the Waiting Pavilion, and the Moon View Arbor. In a place like this one might spend weeks in perfect contentment, enjoying nature and the great art collection.

CATALOGUE

SUMMARY OF CHINESE DYNASTIES

(Mythical and Legendary Periods Omitted)

SAN TAI (or "Three Early Dynasties"):

Hsia	B. C. 2205—1767
Shang	B. C. 1766—1122
Chou	B. C. 1121—255
FEUDAL PERIOD	B. C. 255—221
CH'IN DYNASTY	B. C. 221—206
HAN DYNASTY	B. C. 206—A. D. 25
EASTERN HAN DYNASTY	A. D. 25—221
After HAN	A. D. 221—265

(*Epoch of "Three Kingdoms," viz.:* Han, Wei *and* Wu)

CHIN DYNASTY	A. D. 265—323
EASTERN CHIN DYNASTY	A. D. 323—420

(*Epoch of Division North and South*)

SUNG (House of LIU)	A. D. 420
CH'I	A. D. 479
LIANG	A. D. 502
CHIEN	A. D. 557

SUI DYNASTY	A. D. 581—617
T'ANG DYNASTY	A. D. 618—906

WU TAI (or "Five (Short) Dynasties"):

Posterior Liang		A. D. 907
"	T'ang	A. D. 923
"	Ch'in	A. D. 936
"	Han	A. D. 947
"	Chou	A. D. 951

NORTHERN SUNG DYNASTY	A. D. 960
SOUTHERN SUNG DYNASTY	A. D. 1127—1279
YUAN (MONGOLIAN) DYNASTY	A. D. 1280—1367
TA MING DYNASTY	A. D. 1368—1643
TA CH'ING (TS'ING): MANCHU DYNASTY	A. D. 1644—1911

FIRST AFTERNOON'S SALE

THURSDAY, FEBRUARY 27, 1913

AT THE AMERICAN ART GALLERIES

BEGINNING AT 2.30 O'CLOCK

1—*AMETHYSTINE SNUFF BOTTLE*

Height, 2¼ inches; width, 2 inches.

Flattened tapering form, with scrolled edges in openwork. Obverse and reverse presenting figures of sages. Emerald-colored glass stopper.

2—*SMALL WHITE JADE PLAQUETTE*

Height, 3¾ inches; width, 2⅞ inches.
With stand: Height, 6½ inches.

Oval, with serrated edge and perforations, vertically mounted on teakwood stand. White nephrite of suet-like translucency, so-called "mutton fat" jade; carved with a pair of dragons midst cloud scrolls in low relief. Reverse side sustains scrolling ornament and a channeled groove.

3—*AMETHYSTINE SNUFF BOTTLE*

Height, 2¾ inches; width, 2 inches.

Flattened gourd-shape, surrounded by an openwork of scrolling stems, including the small fruit of the gourd. On the obverse the god of happiness, carved in bold relief. Green glass stopper in gourd form.

4—EMERALD-GREEN JADEITE BUCKLE

Length, 4 inches.

Ancient form of girdle buckle. Rare Imperial *fei-ts'ui* with dragon-like head, and young *shih-lung* dragon midst fungi scrolls. Carved in relief, with openwork and undercutting. The design represents "the celestial dragon guarding its young." Ta Ch'ing Dynasty.

5—TWO SMALL ROCK-CRYSTAL VASES

Height, 4⅜ inches.

Cylindrical shape, the contracted neck sustaining four small looped handles with loose suspended rings. The quartz is flawless and of clear color, with perfect polishing. Have delicate teakwood stands.

6—TWO WHITE JADE PHŒNIX-BIRD BOXES

Height, 4¾ inches; width, 4 inches.

The fabled *fêng* or phœnix birds are standing, with crested heads, and floral twigs below their beaks, the lower parts of the bodies forming boxes resting on the birds' legs, and the upper part being removable as covers. Sculptured from white nephrite, the so-called "mutton fat" jade, of even color and translucent. Heads turned to right and left, respectively. Ta Ch'ing Dynasty.

7—GREEN JADEITE VASE WITH COVER

Height, 5¾ inches; width, 2¼ inches.

Graceful ovated shape, flattened, with contracted neck and two elephant-head handles which hold loose rings. Fashioned in green and white blended *fei-ts'ui* (jadeite), of the variety poetically known as "moss entangled with melting snow." The obverse carving in relief depicts a *fêng* (phœnix), and a flowering orchid growing near rocks. Domed cover, of like material, has a simple elongated knob. Ta Ch'ing Dynasty.

8—WHITE JADE SITTING BIRD

Height, 3½ inches; length, 5½ inches.

Sculptured in natural form to represent a species of pea hen, with crested head and erected rump feathers, the graceful head and plumage being carefully rendered. Late XVIIIth century. Has teakwood stand.

9—AMETHYSTINE QUARTZ DUCK

Height, 3¼ inches; length, 4 inches.

Sculptured in natural form; the quartz showing blended violet and grayish zones. Joined base formed by the web feet. Ta Ch'ing Dynasty. Teakwood stand.

10—WHITE JADE SNUFF BOTTLE

Height, 3¼ inches; width, 2¾ inches.

Conventional ovated shape, fashioned in pure nephrite of the "mutton fat" variety. One side shows gilt inscription and figure of a sage with attendant, under a plum tree, and the other side a second attendant with an ox under a pine tree and a similar gilt inscription. The inscription refers to a scholar of the Ming Dynasty. Date: XVIIIth Century.

11—JADE AND LAPIS-LAZULI ORNAMENT

Height, 3 inches; width, 6 inches.

Representing a boat in form of a tree stump carved in Persian lapis-lazuli with mica or silver-like flecking. The figures in the boat are sculptured in white jade, and include an immortal with a youthful attendant bearing a peach. Carved teakwood stand with wave motif.

12—ROCK-CRYSTAL WINE CUP WITH TRAY

Cup: Height, 2½ inches; diameter, 2½ inches.
Tray: Width, 4½ by 3¼ inches.

Fashioned in flawless crystal quartz, enriched by a peony flower ornament in low relief, and with a small dragon handle.

The shallow tray, in quadrifoliate form, of like flawless material, the underside showing peony flowers to match the cup.

13—JEWELED WHITE JADE INCENSE BOX

Diameter, 2½ inches.

Fashioned in form of a magnolia flower, the petals carefully rendered outside and the interior hollowed. The cover enriched by a series of imperial green jadeite studding. Ta Ch'ing Dynasty. Has teakwood stand.

14—JEWELED WHITE JADE LIBATION CUP

Height, 2½ inches; length, 5½ inches.

In archaic ovate form, with a projecting goat-head handle including ruby studding for the eyes. Concentric scrolls form a border about the rim, followed below by curious serpentine motifs rendered in low relief. The translucent grayish-white nephrite includes slight yellowish markings. Early XVIIIth century. Teakwood stand.

(Illustrated.)

15—LARGE CAMPHOR QUARTZ SEAL

Height, 5½ inches; width, 2½ inches.

On a square base the figure of a horse, standing, with head turned to one side, is carved in the round, the whole being in one piece of material suggesting the texture of European alabaster quartz. The seal, on the bottom of the square block, is surrounded by archaic dragon-scrolls and reads: "Ye Tsze Pin Han Tong Kin," meaning "An Imperial gift."

16—GREEN JADEITE DOUBLE FLOWER COUPE

Height, 3 inches; width, 5½ inches.

Artistically carved to represent a natural campanulate magnolia flower, upstanding, and connected with the sacred fungus at the base; stem and leafage are included. Fine openwork and undercutting, with perfect polishing. Date: XVIIIth century. Ta Ch'ing Dynasty. Has carved ivory stand, the openwork showing bamboo, pine and plum blossom motifs.

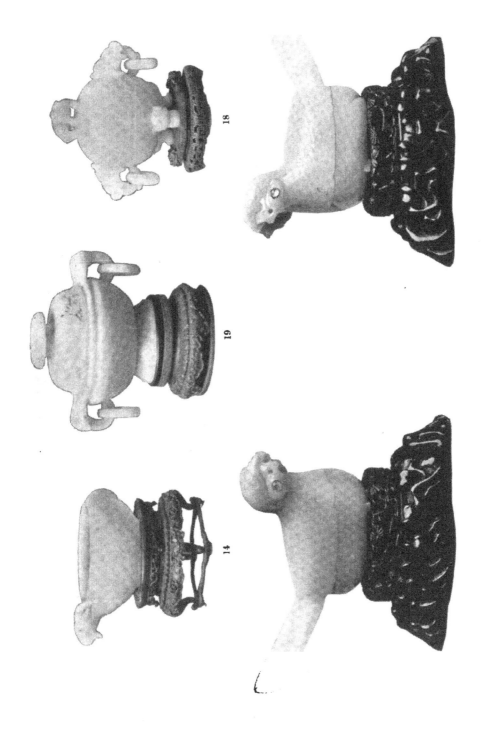

17—GREEN AND GRAY JADEITE BOWL

Height, 2 inches; diameter, 5⅝ inches.

Conventional shape, showing rare emerald clouding and a grayish crystalline structure, with a rare translucency. Flecked with yellowish notes. Fine and interesting example. Ta Ch'ing Dynasty. Has teak-wood stand.

18—PURE WHITE JADE TRIPOD CENSER

Height, 4½ inches; diameter, 3 inches.

Spherical form, with two dragon-head handles and loose rings, on three monster-head feet, the globular body encircled by a horizontal bordering in low relief sustaining archaic gluttonous ogre or *haou-tëen* lineaments copied from ancient bronzes. The cover of like rare material is surmounted by a fabled *ch'i-lin*, a monster of good omen. Date: XVIIIth century. Has teakwood stand with silver wire inlaying.

(Illustrated.)

19—SMALL WHITE JADE INCENSE BURNER .

Height, 4 inches; diameter, 4½ inches.

Shallow round shape with low spreading base, and monster-head handles holding loose rings, the exterior carved in low relief with hieratic scrolls. The base is encircled by a leaf bordering, and the cover by a floral border including *shou* characters and fishes. Cover surmounted by a hollow and gadrooned knob. Ta Ch'ing Dynasty. Has gilt bronze and champlevé enamel stand.

(*Illustrated.*)

20—COURT NECKLACE, OR ROSARY

Composed of numerous dark amber-colored beads with plaques and pendants indicating the rank of the wearer. The string is composed of one hundred and eight of the beads, supplemented by short strings of amethyst, coral, jade, beryl and rose-colored quartz, interrupted by four beads of imperial green jadeite. This necklace was worn by Prince Kung.

21—AMETHYSTINE TRIPOD CENSER

Height, 4¼ inches; width, 4½ inches.

Flattened oval shape with dragon-head handles and free rings. The body is raised on three fungiform feet, and is carved with fungus clumps in low relief. The stone is of a deep violet tone with a band of grayish structure through the center. The small cover, of like material, has a large fungiform knob, in deep carving and undercutting. Date: XVIIIth century.

22—MOSS-GREEN JADE MEDALLION MOUNTED ON STAND

Height, 5¼ inches; with stand, 8 inches.

Presenting a pierced sacrificial emblem (*ku pi*), with archaic dragon ornament, the disk center (an ancient "symbol of heaven") showing hieratic scrolls that involve bird-like forms, together with four characters alluding to the sun, moon, planets and constellations. Attributable to the Ta Ming Dynasty. The teakwood stand carved with bat forms.

23—MOUNTED WHITE JADE BUDDHA IDOL

Height, 5½ inches; width, 3 inches.

Representing one of the Tibetan Bodhisat Triad, probably Pu-hsien, the "All Good," adorned with a tiara and flowing scarf of gilt bronze. Seated in traditional posture, the hands holding a temple vessel. Mounted on a jade thalamus with an escalloped gilt bronze base-rim. Date: XVIIIth century. Has teakwood stand.

24—ORIENTAL AMBER IDOL ON CARVED AMBER BASE

Height, 7½ inches; diameter of base, 3½ inches.

Representing Lao-Tsze, the god of longevity, philosopher, and founder of the Taoist sect. Rendered in long flowing robes of the Chou Dynasty, holding his attribute, the peach, in his right hand, and standing upon a rocky eminence surrounded by waves. Date: XVIIth century. Ta Ming Dynasty.

25—GREEN JADEITE BOWL WITH COVER

Height, 2½ inches; diameter, 5 inches.

Buddhist temple or alms bowl, fashioned in mottled emerald-green *fei-ts'ui* with grayish clouding and of typical translucency. The exterior of the bowl is ornamented with an escalloped fungus-head bordering in low relief that is repeated on the cover, which has a round aperture for the alms. Ta Ch'ing Dynasty. Has elaborate olive-green jade base, with openwork carving.

26—TWO JEWELED WHITE JADE DOVE-SHAPED BOXES

Height, 3¼ inches; width, 6 inches.

The birds are represented with floral sprigs in their beaks, with emerald-green jadeite and rose quartz setting. Sculptured in white (*pai-yü*) nephrite of translucent quality and even color of the "mutton fat" variety. Upper half of the bird, with the head and tail, forms the cover, and the lower the ovoid bowl. Ta Ch'ing Dynasty. Fitted with double teakwood stands.

(Illustrated.)

27—GRAYISH-GREEN JADE HAND REST

Length, 7 inches.

Of oblong form, with curving ends, as if an unrolled parchment scroll, the upper surface carved in sunken relief with hieratic scroll designs involving the admonitory *t'ao t'ieh* ogre lineaments, centered by a circular dragon crest. Era of K'ang-hsi (1662-1722).

28—AMETHYSTINE QUARTZ COUPE

Height, 3½ inches; diameter, 3½ inches.

Sculptured in form of a pomegranate surrounded by foliage, with stems and birds, in bold relief; at one end a reclining figure holding bird. The quartz is a deep violet, with grayish clouding. Early Ta Ch'ing Dynasty. Teakwood stand carved with birds and blossoms.

29—JEWELED WHITE TIBETAN JADE INCENSE BOWL WITH COVER

Height, 3½ inches; diameter, 3¾ inches.

Graceful rounded form with circular base, and two lotus flower handles with openwork carving and ruby incrustations, the sides delicately carved with lancet bordering. The bottom is carved with a conventional stellated flower motif in Indian style. The cover, with foliated border, is surmounted by a floral knob with a ruby setting. Green jade stand, carved and pierced.

30—SEA-GREEN JADEITE BRUSH HOLDER

Height, 5 inches; width, 2½ inches.

Carved to represent a bamboo stalk, and on one side with a phœnix with spreading tail over an openwork rockery. The sea-green *fei-ts'ui* (jadeite) shows emerald-green marking. Young bamboo shoots and floral plants complete the design. Date: XVIIIth century. Has teakwood stand.

31—ORIENTAL AGATE LIBATION COUPE

Height, 2¼ inches; diameter, 5½ inches.

Fashioned in the form of a flower, with petal rim and thinly cut, the handle formed by a clinging dragon with his head reaching the rim and his cleft tail spreading over the base of the body. The material shows rich brown mottling, with translucency and perfect polish. Teakwood stand.

32—GREENISH-WHITE JADE SCEPTER

Length, 12½ inches.

Conventional form, with head-piece carved in archaic scrolling details and a unique example of the *shou* character of longevity. The flattened rod or handle is carved with a small *shih-lung* (dragon) in bold relief and a lotus-flower motif, and the pointed lower end has iron-red markings. Date: XVIIth century.

33—WHITE JADE BOWL

Diameter, 5¼ inches.

Fashioned in translucent white nephrite (*pai-yü*) of even quality. The exterior carved in low relief with conventional foliated borders at rim and base. Thinly cut and uniformly finished by soft polishing. Date: XVIIIth century. Carved and inlaid teakwood stand.

34—JADEITE VASE GROUP WITH COVERS

Height, 5¾ inches; width, 2¾ inches.

A double vase, or pair of small vases, of slender tapering form, with small handles and rudimentary stands, carved as one piece from a single mass of blended emerald-green and grayish-white jadeite (*fei-ts'ui*). The carving in relief presents a dragon encircling the shoulder of both vases, an emerald-green zone being utilized by the lapidary to form the head of the dragon. The two covers, of dome-shape, are held together by a loose-linked chain, both covers and chain carved from a single piece and detachable from the vases. Ta Ch'ing Dynasty. Has a separate teakwood stand.

35—ROCK-CRYSTAL VASE WITH COVER AND STAND

Height, 8 inches; diameter, 3 inches.

Graceful rounded form, with attenuated neck supporting four looped handles which include loose rings; the surfaces of the vase without ornament. Dome-shaped cover sustaining three dragon-head handles with loose rings and a round knob. Material of flawless quality and brilliant under perfect polishing. The crystal stand fashioned in conventional form.

36—RARE MALACHITE VASE

Height, 6 inches; width, 3¼ inches.

In form of tree stump with openwork boughs and foliation, and a pair of storks carved in full relief, the rich material showing light and dark tones and fine polishing. Has teakwood stand.

37—YELLOWISH-GRAY JADE LIBATION CUP AND SALVER

Cup: Height, 2½ inches; width, 4 inches.
Group: Height, 4 inches; length, 6½ inches.

Fashioned in an ancient design of a loving cup, with two boldly carved dragons forming the handles, their heads projecting over the rim and their serpentine bodies sustaining suspended rings. Remaining surface without ornament, plainly polished. The salver, of rounded quadrilateral form, is of a darker, slaty-gray jade, with an ornamented central baluster as a support for the cup, and a Greek fret border engraved on the flat rim. Date of cup, XVIIth century; of tray, era of Ch'ien-lung.

38—SMALL WHITE AND BLACK JADE MOUNTAIN

Height, 5¼ inches; width, 5 inches.

Carved ancient nephrite boulder; representing a landscape, half of which shows black markings of rare variety. Obverse sustains a stag and doe in bold relief, closely grouped, the accessories including an old pine tree and bare cliffs. Reverse holds a crane standing close to a small brook; the remaining details include rugged cliffs, together with an old pine tree. Date uncertain. Has teakwood stand.

39—GREEN JADEITE VASE OF INCENSE-BURNER FORM

Height, 5 inches; width, 4½ inches; diameter, 3½ inches.

Fashioned in tripod shape, with dragon-head handles and loose rings. The rounded body, on low monster-head feet, is carved with hieratic motifs in relief, showing the lineaments of the *t'ao t'ieh yên* ogre, which are repeated on the cover. The cover sustains also a coiled dragon and three loops with rings. The material, with blended deep and light sea-green tones, shows translucence and rare quality. Ta Ch'ing Dynasty. Has teakwood stand.

40—TRANSLUCENT GRAYISH-WHITE JADEITE TRAY

Length, 7½ inches; width, 5½ inches.

Fashioned in quadrifoliate form with a fret border at the rim, the sunken interior panel displaying young dragons, cloud patches and emblematic bats, beautifully executed. Granular texture and even color. Era of Ch'ien-lung. Openwork teakwood stand.

41—SEA-GREEN JADE TRIPOD

Height, 7 inches; width, 5 inches.

Flattened oviform shape with two boldly carved horned dragon handles from which loose rings depend, on three slender, curving feet with lion masks at the knees. The embellishment of the body includes a descending leaf band under a fretted band, above which appears a hieratic design involving *t'ao t'ieh* lineaments. Has teakwood stand.

42—BLENDED WHITE JADE INCENSE BURNER WITH COVER

Height, 4½ inches; diameter, 4½ inches.

Shallow rounded form, with low base, and two floral handles in openwork carving sustaining loose rings. The exterior carved with a conventional lotus flower motif in delicate relief. The domed cover, with similar carving, is pierced within its open, crcular knob. **Date:** Ch'ien-lung period (1736-1795). Has rock-crystal stand with conventional openwork cutting.

43—GREEN CRYSTAL QUARTZ VASE, WITH FIGURES

Height, 5 inches; width, 4 inches.

Carved in ovoid form within a triangle, and with figures of a sage with his boy attendant, accompanied by a flying crane, a bird and a deer. The composition includes the symbolical pine tree, boldly carved and in free relief. The material shows an aquamarine tone of clear quality. Carved and ivory-studded teakwood stand.

44—WHITE JADE SCHOLAR'S SET

A: *Round Incense Burner*, with pierced and upturned handles, the exterior surface ornamented in low relief with a hieratic motif and admonitory ogre lineaments, followed around the base by an undulating bordering which is repeated on the cover. The latter, which includes a row of gadroon forms, is finished by an openwork and undercut dragon knob.

Height, 4½ inches; width, 6¼ inches.

B: *Flattened Slender Vase*, to hold implements used for handling incense, the carved obverse and reverse presenting archaic dragon motifs and the neck a band of spear heads, in low relief.

Height, 4¼ inches; width, 2 inches.

C: *Small Incense Box*, in quadrifoliate shape, to hold prepared perfumes for burning; a small lotus motif in low relief carved in the central panel of the cover. Date: XVIIIth century.

Height, 2½ inches; diameter, 2½ by 2½ inches.

Each fitted with a teakwood stand.

45—GRAY AND GREEN JADEITE BOWL

Height, 3 inches; diameter, 5½ inches.

Conventional shape, without ornament; fashioned in grayish-white jadeite (*fei-ts'ui*) which shows a slight moss-green flecking, with crystalline translucency and an interesting quality. Ta Ch'ing Dynasty. Has teakwood stand.

Incense burner in rounded tripod form, sculptured with monster-head handles holding loose rings. Raised upon three feet with mask-like knees. Cover sustaining three animal-head handles with loose rings, and a carved knob.

Height, 4¼ inches; width, 5 inches.

Vase of flattened form, with contracted neck sustaining similar handles with loose rings; cover with a flat elongated button top.

Height, 5¼ inches; width, 2 inches.

Incense box of rounded form, on a low circular base, the flawless material showing perfect polish throughout. Each has carved teakwood stand.

Height, 1½ inches; diameter, 2 inches.

47—*WHITE JADE INCENSE BOWL WITH COVER*

Height, 4 inches with cover; diameter, 5 inches.

Squat and rounded form, of thinly cut "Indian School" or Tibetan jade, the exterior showing ornate, melon-like ribbing, with leaf-scroll borders above and below. The entire bottom is carved as a single panel with a stellated center and plume patterns. The ornate cover has four loose rings, an openwork fungiform finial and an escalloped bordering. Date: XVIIIth century. Has teakwood stand.

·

48—*WHITE JADE PLATE*

Diameter, 6 inches.

Of low, hollowed form, thin, and cut from a block of white (*pai yü*) nephrite showing granular structure with a slight grayish flecking. Interior and exterior plainly finished with perfect polishing, bringing out the translucency of the material. Date: XVIIIth century. Teakwood stand with red and green ivory inlays.

49—WHITE JADE CABINET VASE WITH COVER

Height, 7¼ inches; width, 5 inches.

Fashioned in flattened rectangular shape, with curved sides, the short receding neck sustaining dragon-head handles and loose suspended rings. All sides presenting archaic scrolled bands with *fêng* or bird heads completing mask-like forms; copied from ancient bronzes. Oblong cover with relief carving and angular projecting top showing a sunken center. Date: XVIIIth century. Has teakwood stand.

50—MALACHITE ORNAMENT .

Height, 5 inches; width, 6¾ inches.

In natural form, showing the concentric markings and rich green tones under a perfect polish. Teakwood stand.

51—COLLECTION OF TOMB JADE ORNAMENTS

Height, with stand, 8¼ inches; 7¼ inches square.

Twelve small examples, enclosed in a glass case, including human figures, birds and animals. Some appear to have been zodiacal symbols, and others amulets. The varied deep-colored jades stained through long entombment. Han Dynasty. Teakwood stand with glass cover.

52—WHITE JADE VASE WITH COVER

Height, 7 inches; diameter, 4 inches.

Flattened ovated shape, presenting boldly carved plum trees on either side, with branches and birds in full relief and undercutting, the design including a pair of small birds. The white nephrite (*pai-yü*) shows a slight tinge of the sea-green tone. The small cover, of like material, is finished with a simple knob. Date: XVIIIth century.

53—WHITE JADE JU-I, OR SCEPTER

Length, 13 inches.

Conventional curved form, with head-piece showing a branch of a peach tree, carved in low relief and including fruit, blossoms and leafage. The handle, with similar low relief carving, presents bamboo and pine trees, together with flowers, and fungus motifs. On the reverse some bats appear. Fashioned in greenish-white jade (nephrite), with a slight yellowish flecking. Era of Ch-ien-lung (1736-1795).

54—WHITE JADE ELEPHANT CENSER

Height, 5⅜ inches; width. 5¾ inches.

An elephant with trappings and carrying a detachable vase, which forms the cover, is being adorned with emblems by two boyish attendants. The lotus-flowered saddle-cloth has a fret bordering and bat forms. Sculptured in greenish-white (*pai-yü*) nephrite, with yellowish tones. Elephants having served in the past as tribute bearers, with gifts to the Emperor's court, are frequently used as ornaments. Date: XVIIIth century. Has teakwood stand carved with pine and bamboo twigs.

55—MOSS-GREEN JADEITE SCHOLAR'S SET

Fashioned from blended moss-green nephrite (*pai-yü*) with dark gray and emerald tones. For a library shrine.

A: *Round Incense Burner*, with conventional carved monster-head handles. Cover showing delicate pierced lotus flower design, with a carved and corded knob. Date: XVIIIth century.

Height, 5 inches; width, 8½ inches.

B: *Flattened Vase*, to hold small implements for preparing incense, the contracted neck sustaining small recurved handles and the sides archaic carving in low relief, with *haou tëen* masks and escalloped borderings.

Height, 6 inches; width, 3 inches.

C: *Round Incense Box*. Cover carved with a coiled *shih-lung* dragon.

Diameter, 3 inches.

Carved stand for each.

56—GREEN JADEITE VASE WITH COVER

Height, 7½ inches; width, 3 inches.

Graceful ovate shape, flattened, with contracted neck supporting
looped fungiform handles and loose rings. Fashioned in a variety of
jadeite (*fei-ts'ui*) termed by the Chinese *hua hsueh tai tsao* or "moss
entangled in melting snow." Embellished with a pair of dragons in
bold relief, showing emerald tones where the color of the stone deepens.
The cover, carved with a fungus design, includes a dragon knob. Date:
XVIIIth century. Ta Ch'ing Dynasty. Teakwood stand with silver
wire inlaying.

57—RARE OLIVE-GREEN JADE WINE EWER

Height, 6¾ inches; width, 6 inches.

Fashioned in the unique form of an ancient bronze sacrificial vessel, with cover and protruding rim-spout. The body, with fluted sides, sustains two bird-shaped handles, broadly carved and pierced. The curved cover has projecting knobs and archaic ornamentation in low relief and is surmounted by a dragon in conventional form, pierced and in bold relief. The moss-green (*pai-yü*) nephrite shows even color and lustrous quality, with perfect finish. Date: Early XVIIIth century. Has carved teakwood stand.

58—WHITE JADE MARRIAGE BOWL

Height, 2 inches; diameter, 6 inches.

Round, shallow form, fashioned of translucent jade with very slight greenish tones. The carved embellishment of the exterior presents conventionalized lotus scrolls, and representations of the *shuang-hsi* characters, symbolical of wedded joy, four times repeated. The interior displays a pair of fish, emblems of domestic felicity, carved in relief amidst sprays of water weeds. Underneath the foot is a seal mark. Era of Ch'ien-lung (1736-1795). Has teakwood stand.

59—WHITE TIBETAN JADE LIBATION CUP

Height, 2¾ inches; width, 9 inches.

Archaic shape with protruding lip and swan's-neck handle. The exterior enriched with a stellated band and blossoms in conventional Indian School style. Greenish-white tone, with thinly cut sides and beautiful polishing. Date: XVIIth century. Ta Ch'ing Dynasty. Carved coral-colored ivory and teakwood stand.

60—JEWELED WHITE JADE DRAGON CUP

Height, 3½ inches; width, 7¼ inches.

Fashioned of grayish-white nephrite in archaic form of a libation vessel, presenting a pair of *shih-lung* dragons, with bifurcate tails, which form handles, the dragons being done in the round. A third and smaller dragon appears in relief on one side of the rim. The eyes of all three are incrusted with ruby-like stones. Ta Ch'ing Dynasty. Has teakwood stand carved with dragons.

61—SMALL WHITE JADE BOX WITH CHAIN

Height, 1½ inches; length, 6½ inches.

Unique elongated melon-shape, fashioned of pure white nephrite of translucent and flawless quality, a typical example of the so-called "mutton fat" jade. Stems and vines are carved in relief and openwork, and delicately rounded undercutting. The two sections are held together by a short-linked chain, the whole carved from one mass. Interior surfaces show a frog and a lotus plant motif carved in bold relief. Date: XVIIIth century. Teakwood stand carved with vine and fruit motifs.

62—*RARE BLENDED GREEN JADEITE VASE WITH COVER*

Height, 7⅞ inches; width, 3¼ inches.

Flattened rectangular form with curved contour, and contracted neck which sustains two dragon-head handles and loose rings. Carved obverse and reverse surfaces presenting hieratic scrolls which involve *haou tëen* lineaments, the eyes and nose well defined. The neck is surrounded by a border of descending leafage, and the base with small gadroon band. Dome-shaped cover, of like material, surmounted by a simple knob. Ta Ch'ing Dynasty. Has teakwood stand.

63—UNIQUE ARTICULATED WHITE JADE FLOWER VASE

Height, 5½ inches; diameter, 3½ inches.

Graceful interlocked biberon (*mei p'ing*) shape, of grayish-white nephrite with suet-like translucency. Openwork and movable articulation presents dragon scrolls derived from archaic bronze designs, the outlines carved and with sunken details. On the shoulder, suggesting a rudimentary handle, is a phœnix-bird, with plumage delicately rendered in relief, and a dragon in pursuit of the flaming orb amid cloud forms sprawls on the opposite side of the vase. This imperial vase, with scalloped upper rim and raised on three feet formed by small goats, contains an inner vessel of silver. Early XVIIIth century. Teakwood stand.

64—DARK GREEN JADE BOWL

Diameter, 7¾ inches.

Shallow shape with plain circular rim. Thinly fashioned after the famed Yung-lo porcelain bowls of the Ming period. Translucent dark green (*pai-yü*) nephrite with gray and black flecking, approaching rare choromelanite. Perfect polishing. Has teakwood stand with green ivory insets.

65—TWO MOSS-GREEN JADE BOWLS WITH COVERS

Height, 3½ inches with cover; diameter, 5 inches.

Thinly cut, the blended green and gray (*pai-yü*) nephrite here is a dark variety of jade, known as "moss entangled with melting snow." The exterior decoration, in graven form, displays floral and symbolical fruit motifs, including pomegranate and "hand of Buddha" citron, arranged in separate groups. The dome-shaped cover sustains similar symbolical fruit and flower motifs. Date: XVIIIth century. Have carved teakwood stands.

66—JEWELED WHITE JADE ANIMAL GROUP

Height, 3½ inches; length, 5 inches.

Representing three goats, emblems of the springtide revival, carved from one mass of rare white nephrite, with suet-like translucency. On the back of the larger animal appears a spherical jewel on cloud strata. The carving is admirably done. The goats have green jadeite and ruby eyes. Fitted with a double stand.

67—TABLE SCREEN IN FORM OF A WHITE JADE DISK

Diameter, 6½ inches; height, with stand, 11¼ inches.

The carving on the obverse presents a landscape subject, with ploughing scene including a water buffalo, pine trees, habitations, and the figure of a sage attended by boy. The reverse shows another landscape scene with habitations and the figures of three females, occupied with threading cotton or silk. The accessories, including trees, hills and bridges, are beautifully rendered and undercut. Date: XVIIIth century.

68—SMALL ROCK-CRYSTAL WINE POT

Height, 5 inches; length, 8 inches.

Globular body and bird spout, the wings of the bird partly encircling the vessel. Grip handle cut in the form of a young dragon, holding a crystal chain which is linked to the cover. The whole carved from one mass of flawless rock crystal quartz. Perfect polishing. The embellishment includes symbolical fruit trees, representative of the three abundances—of years, sons and happiness.

69—SMALL WHITE JADE WINE EWER

Height, 6¼ inches; diameter, 5½ inches.

Graceful flattened form with slender neck, a curved dragon handle, and a long spout springing from a rudimentary monster-mask at the side. The body surrounded by a border of petal-formed ribbing, reaching up to the middle. The small cover has a meander band at the rim, matching the lower flanges of vessel. Imperial mark. Era of Ch'ien-lung. Teakwood stand.

70—JEWELED WHITE JADEITE TRIPOD

Height, 5½ inches; width, 6½ inches.

Low bulbous shape with two broad upturned handles in curving
and angular form. Raised on three carved monster-head feet, the eyes
studded with green jadeite. The body is intricately carved with hieratic
scrolls, involving *t'ao t'ieh yên*, lineaments of the admonitory ogre, in
low relief. Dome-shaped cover, showing three small oblong vignettes
with scrolling motifs alternately with three recumbent goats, the crowning rim enriched with a row of sapphires, rubies and pearls. Date:
XVIIIth century. Has carved teakwood stand.

71—GRAYISH-WHITE JADE BUDDHA

Height, 6½ inches; width, 4¾ inches.

Representing Amitâbha Buddha, of the Mahâyâna School, seated with crossed legs, in traditional attitude, the hands resting on the knees with palms upward. Head with short curly hair and long ear lobes. Wearing a rosary and the canonical robes of an early epoch. Date: XVIIth century. Teakwood stand carved to represent a lotus throne or thalamus.

72—WHITE JADE WINE EWER WITH COVER

Height, 7¼ inches; width, 5½ inches.

Fashioned of greenish-white nephrite in the form of an ancient tripod, with a curved monster-head handle and a spout in the form of a bird's head. The surface shows the lineaments of the *t'ao t'ieh yên*, or gluttonous ogre, which are repeated in the three tapering coalescent legs. The domed cover is carved with a bulbous blossom knob and foliated side bordering. Ta Ch'ing Dynasty. Has teakwood stand.

73—SEA-GREEN JADEITE BRUSH HOLDER

Height, 5¾ inches; width, 4 inches.

In rustic form of two bamboo stalks joined together, and surrounded by carvings of a phœnix, flowers, a rockery, and fungus clumps, artistically rendered, with openwork and undercutting. The sea-green *fei-ts'ui* shows emerald-green clouding. Young bamboo shoots and twigs with small leafage complete the list of realistic forms. Interiors hollowed for use as brush holders. Date: XVIIIth century. Ta Ch'ing Dynasty. Has teakwood stand.

74—WHITE JADE JU-I, OR SCEPTER

Length, 15¼ inches.

The curved wand, with foliated head-piece of conventional shape, sustaining peach and bat motifs carved in low relief, symbolizing longevity and happiness. The upper side of the flat handle presents a peach tree bearing fruit, together with a bat, and the reverse shows numerous other bats. White-toned jade-nephrite showing yellowish clouding and veining. Has red silk cord with tasseled attachment. Ta Ch'ing Dynasty. Era of Ch'ien-lung (1736-1795).

76—TWO LIGHT SEA-GREEN JADE BOWLS

Height, 2½ inches; diameter, 5¼ inches.

Conventional Eastern form, with thinly cut sides, the exterior presenting one hundred lightly engraved and gilded *shou* marks of longevity. Enclosed above by a swastika-fretted rim-border, and below by a flowered gadroon motif which surrounds the base; interior plainly polished. Date: XVIIth century. Tall teakwood stands.

77—AMETHYSTINE QUARTZ ORNAMENT

Height, 5 inches; width, 5 inches.

Form of pomegranate, with two bats; obverse showing light violet tones; reverse revealing a camphor-like structure, carved in foliage and stem forms. Carved stand.

78—RARE YELLOW JADE VASE GROUP

Height, 7 inches; width, 5 inches.

An ovated jar with cover and small handles, grouped, with a
"*fu* lion" and supported upon a low stand of conventional design, the
stand hollowed and presenting carved sides. The combination fashioned in yellow (*yü ch'in*) nephrite of exceptional rarity. Obverse and
reverse ornamented in low relief with archaic dragon scrolls and mask-
like lineaments. Small cover surmounted by a young lion. Date:
XVIIIth century. Teakwood stand, with silver inlay.

79—*JEWELED JADE BODHISATTVA IMAGE*

Height, 8 inches; width, 3½ inches.

Representing a celebrated Buddhist monk, *T'ang Sêng*, of the VIIth century, a standing figure clad in flowing canonical robes of the period, with a rosary of green incrusted beads surrounding the neck, the hands holding a twig. The forehead bears the *urna* mark in ruby. The teakwood stand, with gilt bronze mounting, includes a reticulated jade *sungar* (arched back-plaque) of intricate scroll design, centered by four characters giving the name. Date: XVIIth century.

80—WHITE JADE VASE WITH COVER

Height, 10 inches with cover; width, 4⅜ inches.

Graceful ovated shape with contracted neck and two small delicately curved handles. Fashioned from pure white (*pai-yü*) nephrite, translucent and showing rare granular structure. Carved with a wide band enclosing a pair of dragons in pursuit of the effulgent jewel, with a *shou* emblem at the center of either side. Small leaf and fret border below, and the whole imposed upon a grill stand carved in the same block of jade. Dome-shaped cover surmounted by a pair of dragons, in openwork carving. Date: XVIIIth century.

81—WHITE JADE HORSE

Height, 4½ inches; length, 8 inches.

A running horse is represented amongst convoluted scrolling clouds, with an ornate saddle cloth, and bearing on his back a small temple resting on a thalamus. Sculptured in white nephrite with slight yellowish veining. Eyes of ruby-colored stones. An ornament of "good omen." Ta Ch'ing Dynasty. Teakwood stand with openwork carving.

82—WHITE JADE ANIMAL GROUP

Height, 4½ inches; width, 6 inches.

Representing a group of three goats couchant, sculptured in white jade of suet-like translucency, with ruby- and emerald-color eyes, closely huddled together and supporting the *yang-yin* emblem on clouds. Ta Ch'ing Dynasty. Has open teakwood stand.

83—BLENDED WHITE JADE CEREMONIAL EWER

Height, 4 inches; width, 8½ inches.

Low elongated form with broad spout and projecting grip handle, with a flattened upper surface showing a hieratic motif, with *t'ao t'ieh* lineaments in low relief. Carved with a series of borders which enclose phœnix-birds and archaic dragon scrolls, copied from ancient bronzes and beautifully rendered in low relief. Attributable to the T'ang or Sung Dynasty. Has teakwood stand.

84—WHITE JADE DUCK GROUP

Height, 4 inches; width, 7½ inches.

A large and a small mandarin duck are represented resting close together; the larger, holding a twig of lotus blossom in its beak, has ruby eyes, set *en cabochon*, whilst the smaller has emerald-colored eyes. The jade is translucent and shows a slight greenish tinge. Date: XVIIIth century. Has teakwood stand.

85—LIGHT GREEN JADEITE RUSTIC VASE

Height, 7 inches; width, 3 inches.

Unique tapering form, fashioned in blended sea-green and white jadeite to represent a rocky cliff, with relief and openwork carving showing pine trees, a waterfall and fungus clumps, deeply rendered with undercutting. Double aperture for flowers. Date: XVIIIth century. Ta Ch'ing Dynasty. Has teakwood stand.

86—WHITE JADE BOWL

Height, 3½ inches; diameter, 6½ inches.

Form of temple alms vessel, presenting a rounded body and spreading neck, the upper rim of which is incrusted with ruby- and emerald-colored stones. The embellishment includes a series of six allegorical bats carved in the rim. On six carved feet. Date: XVIIIth century. Ta Ch'ing Dynasty. Has teakwood stand.

87—TIBETAN JADE BOWL

Height, 3 inches; diameter, 7 inches.

Fashioned from translucent white nephrite of granular (camphor-jade) structure, showing slight traces of buff zones near the base. High sloping sides thinly cut, with two projecting handles, flat and of elliptical outline, which are enriched by emerald-green jadeite studding. Date: XVIIIth century. Has teakwood stand.

88—GREEN TIBETAN JADE BOWL

Height, 2 inches; diameter, 7¼ inches.

Thinly fashioned in dark sage-green nephrite (*pai-yü*) with black flecking, approaching a rare variety of choromelanite. Showing perfect lapidary finish, with eight-lobed rim and body, and with two small handles in the form of curled leaves. The base showing a serrated leaf border. Date: XVIIIth century. Has teakwood stand.

89—JEWELED WHITE JADE BOWL WITH COVER

Height, 5½ inches; diameter, 6 inches.

Graceful rounded form, with pierced floral motif, showing delicately carved peony blossoms and leafy scrolls. Narrow rim band of ruby and emerald-colored studding. Dome-shaped cover of similar pierced floral openwork, with a raised peony flower knob. Date: XVIIIth century. Has teakwood stand.

90—*WHITE JADE INCENSE BOWL WITH COVER AND STAND*

Height, 4⅜ inches; width, 8 inches.

Fashioned in archaic form with vertical dentated ridges and dragon-head handles with loops enclosing rings. The paneling between the lateral ridges is carved in low relief with ogre-mask lineaments. The domed cover, with similar ridges and carving, is surmounted by a coiled dragon which forms the deeply carved knob. White nephrite showing camphor-like structure with translucency. On its own richly ornamented, carved and pierced white jade stand.

91—*RARE RED REALGAR FIGURE*

Height, 11 inches; width, 3½ inches.

Representing Lao-Tsze deified; also known as Shou Lao. The figure, in standing position, holds a peach and a fungus-form scepter in his hands. Fashioned in a light and dark mosaic of realgar. Date uncertain. With carved teakwood stand.

92—TWO MOSS-GREEN JADE BOWLS

Height, 2½ inches; diameter, 7 inches.

Fashioned in conventional rounded shape, the exterior presenting a lotus flower motif with scrolling foliation carved in low relief. Base sustains a small gadroon bordering. Uniformly polished, with plain interior. Date: XVIIIth century. Carved combination teak and box-wood stands.

93—WHITE JADE DUCK GROUP

Height, 3¼ inches; width, 9½ inches.

Representing a pair of mandarin ducks resting upon a large lotus leaf, each holding a lotus stem and bud in its beak. The jade, of suet-like translucency and even quality, shows a slight greenish tinge. The eyes of the ducks are studded with emerald-colored stones, *en cabochon.* Date: XVIIIth century. Has teakwood stand.

94—JEWELED JADE TRIPOD CENSER WITH COVER

Height, 6½ inches; diameter, 5⅛ inches.

Globular form, fashioned in light green *fei-ts'ui,* sustaining two upturned monster-head handles with ruby-colored eyes. On three curved feet, with carved monster heads having ruby-colored eyes. The body is surrounded by a series of bands with ruby studding in two rows. The cover, of similar white jade, displays reticulated carving and ruby studding, and is surmounted by a grotesque lion, carved in standing form. Ta Ch'ing Dynasty. Has teakwood stand.

95—WHITE JADE FLOWER VASE

Height, 8 inches; diameter, 3½ inches.

Fashioned in rustic form with openwork carving, including the eight Taoist immortals accompanied by five bats and a deer. The upper section includes cloud patches, and the base holds a dragon in quest of the jewel of omnipotence. Close by appear the pointed rocks of the "dragon gate rapids." Early XVIIIth century. Has teakwood stand.

96—WHITE JADE INCENSE BOWL WITH COVER

Height, 7½ inches; width, 7 inches.

Flattened ovoid shape with the imbricated petals of a flower forming its body, which rises amidst clustered stems, buds and foliations delicately rendered in elaborate openwork and undercut carving. White nephrite showing a grayish-green tinge. Exterior of bowl sustains four bats, while a fifth appears below, among the stems. Cover similarly carved and surmounted by a chrysanthemum blossom. Date: XVIIIth century. Teakwood stand with openwork carving.

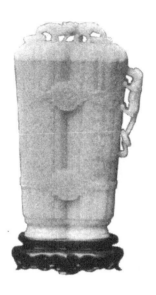

97—WHITE JADE DOUBLE VASE

Height, 8 inches; width, 4½ inches.

Slender cylindrical dual form, tapering downwards, with *shih-lung* (dragon) handles at the sides, these having small free rings, the exterior embellishment showing two bands carved with *shou* cartouches and symbolical pendants held by bats, and also tassels and small swastika forms. Carved jade cover surmounted by a dragon knob. Date: XVIIIth century. Has teakwood stand.

98—WHITE JADE HOUSE BOAT

Height, 4¼ inches; length, 10 inches.

A pleasure craft with the deck-house in three open divisions, with side railings. Figures of a mandarin and boatmen and others are carved in free relief, leaning on the fretted guard rails or moving about in the several open divisions of the craft. The accessories include spars, anchor and large steering oar. Matting is stored on the upper deck, where a small bird has alighted, and a jardinière with a plant stands nearby. The boat is carved 'midst wave forms at the sides, and stern bears an incised gilt inscription, "specially made, era of Ch'ien-lung" (1736-1795). Ta Ch'ing Dynasty. Has teakwood stand carved to represent waves and aquatic plants midst which appear white jade sea-birds.

99—EMERALD-GREEN JADEITE VASE WITH COVER

Height, 8¼ inches; width, 4 inches.

Graceful flattened rectangular shape with receding neck supporting two elephant-head handles, the looped trunks holding rings.
Fashioned in translucent green jadeite with grayish-white, emerald-
green and black markings. Obverse carved in low relief with a dragon
rising from the waves; the reverse with a peony tree, flowers and a
phœnix. Descending leaf border at neck and a fret meander at base.
Cover sustaining an archaic ornament and surmounted by a lion with a
sphere emblem. Date: XVIIIth century. Ta Ch'ing Dynasty. Teakwood stand with silver wire inlaying.

100—*WHITE JADE BIRD VASE WITH COVER*

Height, 9 inches; width, 4¾ inches.

Fashioned of white nephrite in the form of an ancient bronze sacrificial wine vessel, of the shape known as *ch'in ch'ê tsun*, representing a grotesque bird carrying an ornate vase with handles. The curved plumage of the tail forms a part of the support. Domed cover carved with floral buds and two small rings. Date: XVIIIth century. Teakwood stand inlaid with silver wire.

101—WHITE JADE WINE EWER WITH COVER

Height, 8¾ inches; width, 4⅜ inches.

Conventional bottle shape, with cylindrical neck, cornice spout, and a recurved handle which reaches from shoulder to rim of neck. *Shih-lung* or lizard-like dragons with cleft tails, sculptured in bold relief and having jeweled eyes, disport about the body of the vase, which shows slight yellowish veining. The cover of like material is surmounted by a coiled dragon. Ta Ch'ing Dynasty. Has teakwood stand inlaid with silver wire.

102—WHITE JADE HANGING JAR WITH COVER

Width, 4½ inches; complete height, 14 inches.

Hexagonal basket form including a linked chain with cross bar, carved from one block of white nephrite (*pai-yü*) of translucent suet-like quality. The body has an openwork top, with loose rings at the six angles, and the sides are delicately carved with archaic dragons on a panelled and stellated ground. Upper rim of neck has openwork carving of Buddhistic emblems and the base is bordered by a fret band. Small cover with arched top showing lotus flowers and seed pods delicately carved in openwork.

Height of jade 8½ inches, with chain. Has teakwood stand with arch hanger.

103—*WHITE JADE PRESENTATION BOWL*

Height, 3¼ inches; diameter, 7 inches; width, including handles, 9½ inches.

Shallow rounded shape with an escalloped rim and two projecting allegorical bat handles with loose rings. On four small bowl-shaped feet; the obverse and reverse displaying peach tree motifs carved in low relief, including fruit and small bats. Interior shows a continuation of the peach tree boughs, with fruit and foliage. The nephrite shows suet-like translucency with very slight greenish tinge. Underneath bears Imperial mark and inscription in gilt of the era of Ch'ienlung. Has inlaid teakwood stand.

104—WHITE JADE JU-I, OR SCEPTER

Length, 16½ inches.

Conventional curved wand with head-piece showing a dragon and wave motif; flat handle bearing a presentation inscription from the Emperor Ch'ien-lung. The end of the rod is embellished with a small pine tree design in low relief. Light céladon tone. Era of Ch'ien-lung (1736-1795).

105—GRAYISH-WHITE JADE DISK WITH TEAKWOOD MOUNTING

Diameter, 6¾ inches; with stand, complete height, 11½ inches.

Forming a small table screen; the circular panel with carving in low relief, presenting a floral motif in free rendering, the flowers resembling orchids. Grayish-white nephrite with a slight flecking, softly polished, and of waxy texture. Reverse finished with a rim border in key fret pattern.

106—WHITE JADE VASE WITH COVER

Height, 7¾ inches; width, 4½ inches.

Flattened ovate shape with contracted neck. The obverse sustaining a plum (*mei*) tree motif in bold relief with elaborate openwork and undercutting, the reverse showing a species of plant in like relief, growing in rocky soil. Plain cover with small knob. Date: XVIIIth century. Has teakwood stand.

107—WHITE JADE VASE WITH COVER

Height, 8½ inches; width, 3⅝ inches.

Flattened ovate shape with contracted neck and two angular handles. On all sides lotus flower motifs carved in bold relief and undercut, with seed-pods and foliage. A flying bird appears hovering above the flowers. The base sustains a wave pattern and the cover is plainly polished and surmounted by a simple knob. Date: XVIIIth century. Has carved stand.

108—*ROCK-CRYSTAL WINE POT WITH CHAIN AND COVER*

Height, 5½ inches; width, 10 inches.

Globular body, with a phœnix spout and dragon-head handle, carved with symbolical fruits of the abundances, the pomegranate, peach and hand-of-Buddha citron, with foliation and stems. Small cover with nine links of chain connecting it with the handle. Fashioned from one mass of flawless rock-crystal quartz, brilliant under the perfect polishing. Has teakwood stand.

109—LARGE WHITE JADE COUPE

Height, 3 inches; diameter, 6¼ inches.

In shape of an alms bowl with flattened top. Mutton-suet texture, the exterior carved in bold relief with five large bats (*wu fü*) disporting among clouds. The rim is enriched by a lanceolated fungiform border and the base by a conventional wave pattern. Bears Imperial seal. Era of Ch'ien-lung (1736-1795).

˙110—*EMERALD-GREEN JADEITE VASE WITH COVER*

Height, 8½ inches; width, 3⅜ inches.

Flattened rectangular shape with receding neck sustaining two conventional bat-like handles with loose rings. Obverse and reverse carved in low relief with angular scrolls and archaic mask-like lineaments copied from ancient bronzes; the narrow sides with *shih-lung* or dragon forms, and the neck and base with imbricated leaf borderings. Cover presenting relief carving to match vase. Ta Ch'ing Dynasty. Has teakwood stand with silver wire inlaying.

111—WHITE JADE TABLE SCREEN

Height, 6 inches; width, 8 inches; complete height, 11 inches.

An oblong slab of grayish-white nephrite presenting a boldly sculptured landscape scene with varied symbolical trees, habitations and rocky ledges, and the eight Taoist immortals (*Pa Hsien*) with their several attributes assembling in the *shou-shan* or mountain retreat. The details are rendered with deep undercutting. Reverse plainly polished. Mounted on carved teakwood stand, including a carved boxwood inset panel with deer and crane. XVIIIth century.

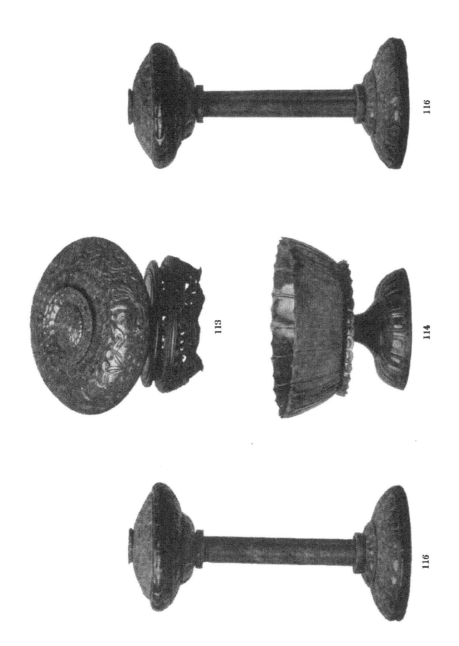

116

113

114

116

112—WHITE JADE INCENSE BOWL WITH COVER

Height, 4¾ inches; diameter, 9 inches.

Low circular form with three butterfly handles with loops and loose rings. Body encircled by a narrow band carved in low relief presenting small archaic scrolls that vaguely suggest the tiger-mark lineaments. The three low feet show archaic monster-heads. The plainly polished cover is surmounted by three carved butterflies forming a knob beneath which are three loose rings. Underneath the foot is an Imperial seal mark. Era of Ch'ien-lung. Has tall gilt bronze stand with floral openwork.

113—TWO MOSS-GREEN JADE ROUND BOXES

Height, 1½ inches; diameter, 7¾ inches.

Low circular form fashioned in blended olive and moss-green nephrite (*pai-yü*) with black flecking. The exteriors uniformly carved in low relief with lotus and scroll foliations, beautifully rendered throughout. The covers showing like floral details in relief, thin cutting and perfect lapidary finish. With teakwood stands.

(Illustrated.)

114—TIBETAN MOSS-GREEN BOWL WITH STEM AND STANDARD

Height, 5¼ inches; diameter, 7¼ inches.

Unique form of a shallow bowl, shaped as a flower, poised on a slender stem which is supported by a low-spreading base; fashioned in one mass of dark-green nephrite, showing black flecking, and of translucent quality like chloromelanite. The sides with the petal ribbing of a lotus flower, which is repeated in the interior, where the bottom is a mass of the protuberant seeds, as a lotus pod. The petal ribbing is repeated on the base. Finely polished. Date: XVIIIth century. Has teakwood stand.

(Illustrated.)

115—MOSS-COLORED JADEITE BOWL WITH COVER

Height, 3¼ inches; diameter, 8¼ inches.

Round shallow shape, thinly cut and beautifully polished; bowl and cover fashioned from a homogeneous mass of dark *fei-ts'ui* of the variety known as "moss entangled with melting snow." The grayish clouding includes a warm buff tone. Ta Ch'ing Dynasty. Has teakwood stand.

116—TWO MOSS-GREEN JADE HAT STANDS WITH SECRET BOXES

Height, 12 inches; diameter, 5½ inches.

The slender fluted stems, raised on carved round bases, are fashioned, like the bases and tops, of dark-green nephrite. The bases show three rows of spiral petals, and the tops, or covers of the box sections, sustain two rows of like petal forms. The box sections themselves are of carved teakwood and the covers hook on by a secret twist. Date: XVIIIth century. On fixed teakwood stands.

(Illustrated.)

117—WHITE JADE PRESENTATION BOWL

Height, 3¾ inches; diameter, 6¼ inches; width between handles, 8 inches.

Artistically fashioned in form of a chrysanthemum flower and supplemented by two carved floral handles showing foliation in delicate openwork design, with undercutting. Exterior finished with double row of imbricated petals which is repeated on the interior with an added spiral formation. Foot underneath bears incised Ch'ien-lung seal mark (1736-1795). Has teakwood stand.

118—ROCK-CRYSTAL DEER GROUP

Length, 10 inches; height with stand, 7 inches.

Presenting a recumbent deer and fawn, together with fungus clumps, symbolizing official honors and long life. Vigorously sculptured, with undercutting and perfect polishing. Teakwood stand, with openwork carving showing pine twigs and blossoms.

119—LIGHT SEA-GREEN JADE VASE

Height, 7½ inches; diameter, 5 inches.

Ovated form with two tubular handles at neck, the flattened surfaces of which show double dragons in bold relief. Obverse and reverse carved in low relief with archaic scrolls involving *hao tëen* lineaments copied from ancient bronzes. On the neck, ascending leafage and fretwork. Date: XVIIth century. Has teakwood stand.

120—*WHITE JADE TABLE SCREEN*

Diameter, 8¼ inches; height, with stand, 14 inches.

A disk of grayish-white (*pai-yü*) nephrite of translucent quality, boldly carved with a landscape subject. The details include the figure of an elderly Taoist sage, with a peach, emblem of long life, who is attended by boy bearing a double fish, a symbol of fidelity, while a crane appears above with the Ch'ing, emblem of rank, in its beak. Reverse plainly polished. Date: XVIIIth century. Mounted on teakwood table.

121—WHITE JADE SCHOLAR'S SET

(In three pieces, to stand before a shrine in the library.)

A: *Tripod Incense Burner* with cover. Carved with ribbed body to represent a chrysanthemum flower. With two floral handles showing elaborate openwork foliations and undercutting. Date: XVIIIth century.

Height, 6½ inches; width, 7 inches.

B: *Slender Vase*, to hold implements for handling the incense. Carved with ribbed body and sustaining flowering chrysanthemum handles with openwork to match the censer.

Height, 6 inches; diameter, 2⅝ by 2 inches.

C: *Small Round Box*, to hold the incense, finished with ribbing and sustaining an elaborate openwork cover.

Height, 2¼ inches; diameter, 3¼ inches.

Fitted with separate stands and a triple base for all.

122—WHITE JADE LARGE SHALLOW BOWL

Height, 3 inches; diameter, 7⅝ inches.

Round, with two elaborate floral handles that show delicate open-work carving and hold free rings. Raised on four tri-lobed feet. The body carved in low relief with small gourds, vines and foliations. Underneath the foot an Imperial mark in four characters, reading "Ch'ien-lung period, specially made." Has teakwood stand.

123—WHITE JADE BEAKER

Height, 7½ inches; width, 5½ inches.

With vertical ribs and slightly flaring many-lobed lip. Curved fungi-clump handles with loose rings. Date: Early XVIIIth century. Has teakwood stand.

124—MOSS-GREEN JADE WINE EWER WITH COVER

Height, 10 inches; width, 6 inches.

Graceful oviform with attenuated neck and recurved leaf-shaped
handle and spout delicately buttressed. Obverse and reverse with low
relief carving presenting lotus flowers and seed cups, and foliations.
The cover with delicate relief carving and a raised knob. Era of Ch'ien-
lung (1736-1795). Ta Ch'ing Dynasty. Has teakwood stand.

125—WHITE JADE TRIPOD INCENSE BOWL

Height, 7 inches; width, 9 inches.

Low globular shape with boldly projecting and vigorously carved
dragon-head handles with loose rings. The body, raised on three low
monster-head feet, sustains archaic and angular scroll motifs in combination with the admonitory lineaments of the gluttonous ogre. Rendered
in low relief. The cover of like material has dragon-scroll carving and
is surmounted by the fabled *ch'i-lin.* Date: XVIIIth century. Has
silver-inlaid teakwood stand.

126—JEWELED WHITE JADE INCENSE URN WITH COVER

Height, 5½ inches; diameter, 8 inches.

Low oval shape with elaborate dome cover. Fashioned in white nephrite of even color and translucent quality. Carved with symbolical bamboo and fungus-clump motifs in low relief and incrusted with semi-precious stones of varied colors in the form of bats, butterflies, Buddha's-hand fruit and floral sprays. Dome cover incrusted with coral, emerald, ruby and green jadeite in varied designs, with a looped top with emerald studding and two suspended rings of jade. Ta Ch'ing Dynasty. Has teakwood stand.

127—WHITE JADE JU-I, OR SCEPTER

Length, 14¾ inches.

Head-piece in conventional shape, carved with Buddhist symbols of happy augury, including a *ch'ing* pendant or sounding stone held by a bat; a fish and a small swastika cross in low relief completing the design. The handle with cloud forms and a group of bats in low relief and highly polished. Lower end sustaining another bat (completing the five-bat or *Wu-fu* motif), together with a ring to hold cord and tassel attachment. Date: XVIIIth century.

128—PAIR OF MOSS-GREEN JADE TABLE SCREENS

Height, 8 inches; height with stand, 12 inches.

Upright oblong panels of green (*pai-yü*) nephrite, boldly carved with picturesque landscape subjects, one including rugged cliffs, bamboo, pine and willow trees, introduced as symbols of long life; the other with a rugged mountain cliff, a cascade and trees. On both, the reverse, plainly polished, bears the so-called "one hundred *shou* characters" of longevity, engraved in gilt in eight rows. Mounted with carved teakwood and boxwood stands. XVIIIth century.

129—MOSS-GREEN JADE LOTUS VASE

Height, 8½ inches; width, 5 inches.

Fashioned in natural form of a lotus leaf, folded and somewhat flattened, upstanding midst stems and with buckling rim, the carving including venation, and leafage and buds in bold relief and undercutting. A small bird has alighted on a stem, while its flying mate appears above. Interior deeply hollowed out to hold water. Date: XVIIIth century. Has carved stand.

130—WHITE JADE RUSTIC VASE

Height, 6 inches; diameter, 6 inches.

Fashioned in form of a large hollowed tree stump, surrounded by small trees, knolls, twigs and a rocky formation, carved and undercut, the white-toned nephrite showing a sea-green tinge and translucent quality. Date: XVIIIth century. Has teakwood stand.

131—GRAY JADE VASE

Height, 8 inches; width, 5 inches.

Hexagonal, with receding neck, two rudimentary mask and ring handles serving as ornaments; the two flattened sections with low relief carving sustaining archaic mask and scroll motifs, the neck presenting figures of boys in bold relief. Shoulder and neck are bordered with fret patterns, and the base has varied diaper patterns in panel form. Date uncertain. Attributable to a pro-T'ang dynasty. Teakwood stand.

132—PAIR OF WHITE JADEITE DISHES

Diameter, 8 inches.

Shallow round shape; fashioned in *fei-ts'ui*, showing a slight tinge of sea-green, with granular structure and typical translucency. Carved exterior presenting borderings of lancet and fret forms in low relief. Interior with a central raised ring of gadroons surrounded by the Buddhistic emblems of happy augury known as the *"pa chi-hsiang"* in low relief. One bearing the Imperial seal mark. Era of Ch'ien-lung (1736-1795). Carved teakwood stands.

133—ROCK-CRYSTAL FIGURE

Height, 12 inches; width, 6 inches.

Representing a female Rishi, Si Wang Mu, queen of the Taoist fairies, rendered in standing form, carrying a spray of peony flowers and accompanied by a phœnix, her aerial steed. On carved teakwood stand.

134—RARE MALACHITE ORNAMENT

Height, 9 inches; width, 7½ inches.

Sculptured to represent a mountainous landscape, with trees and a cascade, and the figure of a priest who is seated on a ledge, holding a rosary. His attendant appears seated below. An inscription on upper right side, in red, indicates that this object was made for the Imperial palace by Yip Low Mo. Has carved teakwood stand with openwork.

135—PINK CORAL FIGURINE

Height, 6¼ inches; with the base, 10 inches; width of base, 9½ inches.

Representing an old sage, carved from the natural material, standing with arms extended and holding a small crystal ball. He is standing on a massive base of natural malachite in the form of a coral reef but retaining its own green hue, and at his side is a larger crystal ball.

136—LAPIS-LAZULI FLOWER VASE

Height, 8 inches; width, 6¼ inches.

Rectilinear, embellished with archaic borderings, and sustaining a large magnolia flower carved in high relief on one side of the narrow sides, with undercutting of the foliage. Upper rim finished with a fret border. Deep blue Persian lapis-lazuli, with a mica speckling and lighter tones; soft polishing. Teakwood stand.

137—ROCK-CRYSTAL VASE WITH COVER

Height, 9½ inches; width, 5¾ inches.

Flattened rectangular form, with attenuated neck supporting monster-headed handles and loose rings. The relief carving presents a pair of dragons amid clouds and sea waves, and the fabled phœnix, a young bamboo and peony flowers. Cover with oblong knob and cloud patches. Has teakwood stand.

138—WHITE JADE VASE WITH COVER

Height, 10⅛ inches; width, 5 inches.

Graceful flattened ovoid shape with low slanting neck sustaining dragon-head handles and loose rings. Downward tapering form of body presenting angular dragon-headed motifs, with archaic scrolls, which vaguely involve the hieratic *t'ao t'ieh* lineaments, copied from ancient bronzes. Dome-shaped cover with sunken knob in elliptic form plainly polished. Date: XVIIIth century. Ta Ch'ing Dynasty. Has teakwood stand.

139—UNIQUE WHITE JADE SWAN VASE

Height, 8⅞ inches; width, 5½ inches.

Fashioned in dual form, with rounded body enclosed by the wings and raised upon the slender legs of two swans, supplemented by delicately carved clustering fungus clumps. The arched necks of the two birds form upper handles, whilst other handles are formed of the sacred *ling-chi* below, with loops holding loose rings. One of the swan's heads is connected by a double-linked chain with the elaborate and tall bell-shaped and openwork cover, which presents other forms of the *ling-chi* fungus clumps and openwork clustering stems. A remarkable example of Chinese lapidary art; cut from one mass of rare nephrite. Ta Ch'ing Dynasty. Has openwork stand of teakwood.

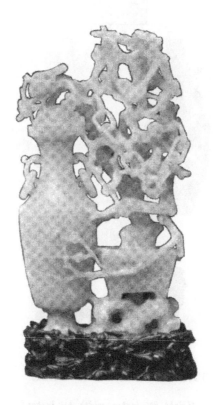

140—WHITE JADE FLOWER VASE GROUPED WITH TREE

Height, 9½ inches; width, 5 inches.

Combination of a slender vase, with a chained cover, and a potted plum tree, with birds and flowers. Fashioned from one mass of limpid white jade showing slight yellowish markings. The vase, enriched by looped handles and loose rings, is joined to the small dwarfed plum tree growing in a low square tub, and a linked chain holds the flower-topped cover—which is surmounted by a bird—to a branch of the tree. Era of Ch'ien-lung (1736-1795).

141—AMETHYSTINE QUARTZ MOUNTAIN

Height, 5½ inches; width, 7½ inches.

Presenting two peaks with holes to hold floral stems, the remaining surfaces suggesting rocky cliffs bare of vegetation. The material has dark violet tones and paler ones toward the sides. Has teakwood stand.

142—MOSS-GREEN JADE VASE WITH COVER

Height, 8½ inches; width, 6 inches.

Graceful oviform with looped handles and loose rings. Boldly carved with a *shih-lung* dragon and a phœnix, with small coalesced vases of bamboo and floral form appearing on the sides, and a dwarfed peach tree in free relief. Cover surmounted by the grotesque "*fu* dog." Date: XVIIIth century. Ta Ch'ing Dynasty. Has teakwood stand.

143—JADE TABLE SCREEN

Height, 8¼ inches; height, with standard, 11¾ inches.

Upright oblong panel with slightly rounded top, of grayish-white (*pai-yü*) nephrite, with iron-red patches. Obverse displaying a mountain scene with rugged cliffs, a waterfall, pine trees, and a lake, and a pleasure boat in which five figures appear. Reverse presents another boldly carved landscape, with lake and a moored boat and three human figures. Mounted on teakwood standard with small green ivory inset panels. XVIIIth century.

144—CLEAR WHITE JADE VASE WITH COVER

Height, 11¼ inches; width, 4¾ inches.

Flattened ovate shape and slender section, the contracted neck sustaining monster-head handles with loose rings. Obverse and reverse with serrated and fretted borders at neck and a gadroon band at the base, while the central surfaces sustain archaic dragon motifs rendered in low relief. The cover, with meander edge and gadroon bands, is surmounted by a couchant monster in openwork carving. Ta Ch'ing Dynasty. Has teakwood stand.

145—WHITE JADE PLUM TREE VASE WITH COVER

Height, 9¾ inches; width, 7 inches.

The vase presenting a flattened oviform contour, with conventional recurved handles, enriched at either end by bold carvings of dwarfed plum trees and fungus clumps (symbolizing long life), vigorously rendered, with openwork and delicately finished undercutting. The dome-shaped cover sustains a bough with clustering plum blossoms. Date: Ta Ch'ing Dynasty. Has teakwood stand with carving and silver inlaying.

146—WHITE JADE TABLE SCREEN

Tablet, 7½ by 7½ inches; total height, 11 inches.

Square slab of grayish-white nephrite, with rounded corners and mounted in a teakwood and ivory stand. Obverse with garden scene, balustraded terraces, a bridge, a stream and a peach tree; a favorite theme. Taoist genii are offering their devotions to Shou Lao, the god of longevity, who appears above, approaching on the back of a huge crane, flying midst cloud strata. The background is composed of mountains and pine trees. Reverse presents a low relief carving in form of cloud scrolls and the five-bat motif. Ta Ch'ing Dynasty.

147—LARGE WHITE JADE JU-I, OR SCEPTER

Length, 16½ inches.

Conventional curved form terminating in a foliated headpiece, with the Three Star Gods carved in low relief. Center plaquette on handle showing a deer; curved end piece carved with a crane under a pine tree. Green silk cord and poly-colored silk tassel attachment. Era of Ch'ienlung (1736-1795).

148—WHITE PEBBLESTONE JADE VASE

Height, 8¾ inches.

Flattened double-gourd shape with two small openwork dragon handles. The rounded surfaces without ornamentation, finely polished to bring out the yellowish-toned veining in this remarkable material. Foot underneath bears a five-character mark, indicating that this example was specially made for the Emperor Ch'ien-lung. Has teakwood stand.

149—SEA-GREEN JADE BEAKER

Height, 9¾ inches; width, 5¼ inches.

With wide and expanded mid-band, narrow base and flaring mouth. The carved embellishment in low relief on center section showing conventional archaic scrolls with *haou tëen* masks; the neck with an ascending lancet border which is reversed on the base. Date: XVIIth century. Teakwood stand.

150—WHITE JADE MOSAIC DISK WITH SIGNS OF THE ZODIAC

Diameter, 11¼ inches.

Fashioned in pure white nephrite of suet-like translucency and rare quality. The various pieces represent a conventionalized flower in twenty-four parts, lying flat. An outer row of segments, with a bordering, shows the twelve animals of the duodenary cycle, represented robed in human form, the reverse sides showing the respective Chinese characters for each. An inner row of spiral-shaped petals, with ancient devices, sustains the twelve emblems used on the robes of the Emperor (restricted to hereditary princes and nobles of the first rank). In the center are the *yang* and *yin* emblems, in light and dark jade, forming a small solid circle of their own, and they separately hold the small "lunar disk" (with hare and pestle) and the "solar disk" (with a bird). All beautifully executed and polished; probably unique. Date: XVIIIth century. Carved teakwood stand with glass case.

151—LIGHT SEA-GREEN JADE VASE WITH COVER

Height, 12¼ inches; width, 5½ inches.

Flattened ovoid form, with lateral dentated ridges, the contracted neck sustaining two dragon handles carved in bold relief and undercutting. The flat surfaces on the body of the vase have low relief carving of archaic dragon scrolls, with the ogre-mask lineaments vaguely defined. Neck with low relief showing a small mountain range, while the base is finished by wave and fret patterns. Cover sustaining coiled dragon clutching the precious orb. Early XVIIIth century. Teakwood stand.

152—WHITE JADE VASE

Height, 8½ inches; diameter, 5 inches.

Flattened oviform with plum (*mei*) trees carved in free relief; branches bearing blossoms spreading over the sides, in openwork and delicately undercut, reaching to the attenuated neck. Cover surmounted by a twisted knob in annular shape. Date: XVIIIth Century. Ta Ch'ing Dyasty. Has teakwood stand.

153—WHITE JADE ELEPHANT AND BOYS

Height, 5½ inches; width, 7½ inches.

Representing the Buddhistic quadruped in miniature, with rich trappings, attended by youths; one at the side bearing a flower vase, and two others with floral twigs on the creature's back. Executed in open-work and undercutting, from one mass of translucent greenish-white (*pai-yü*) nephrite. Date: XVIIIth century.

154—ROCK-CRYSTAL VASE WITH COVER

Height, 10 inches with cover; width, 7 inches.

Flattened oviform, with contracted neck, supporting two monster-head handles and loose rings. Sculptured with deer, pine tree, and crane subjects in high relief and undercutting, the cover supporting a crouching unicorn. Teakwood stand.

155—MALACHITE TABLE SCREEN

Height complete, 13 inches.

An oblong slab of malachite showing inclusions of brilliant lapis-lazuli. An example of great rarity, and therefore mounted without embellishment other than the simple polishing of both sides. The slab measures 7¾ inches by 9. With teakwood stand.

156—JADE RESONANT STONE WITH PENDANTS

Total height, 17½ inches; width, 7 inches.

Consisting of a triangular moss-green jade *ch'ang*, perforated and carved with a pair of dragons and the double-fish emblem, from which depends a middle disk of white jade with piercing, showing a boy and a pomegranate symbol, while the pierced lower pendant of white jade partakes of the form of crossed scepters, looped with fruit. The three objects, joined by gilt chains, are suspended within a teakwood mounting. Ta Ch'ing Dynasty.

157—LARGE WHITE JADE DISH

Diameter, 10 inches.

Deep shape; thinly fashioned from a block of white nephrite (*pai-yü*) showing granular structure with slight grayish flecking. Interior and exterior plainly polished. Date: XVIIIth century. Has tall teakwood stand.

158—MOSS-GREEN JADE VASE

Height, 9¼ inches; diameter, 5¼ inches.

Graceful flattened ovate shape with attenuated neck sustaining two slender tubular handles. The remaining surface, without ornament, presents an unusual blending of emerald and moss-colored green tones with translucency approaching a jadeite quality. Ta Ch'ing Dynasty. Has teakwood stand.

159—SMALL WHITE AND BLACK JADE MOUNTAIN

Height, 6½ inches; width, 7½ inches.

A carved white nephrite boulder, showing black markings. The scenery on the obverse, in bold relief, represents a temple and the habitation or retreat of a sage, who appears on a narrow ledge below, accompanied by a youth. Pine trees, defiles and ledges complete the accessories. Reverse includes trees, a pavilion, deer and a flying crane. Date: Ming Dynasty. Has teakwood stand with openwork carving.

160—TALL AMETHYSTINE QUARTZ VASE WITH COVER

Height, 12¾ inches; diameter, 6 inches.

Fashioned in flattened form with rounded contour, sustaining small lion handles. Body surrounded by "*fu* lions," rendered in free relief, upon rock-shaped ledges and fungus chumps, the carving showing openwork and undercutting. Cover sustains a recumbent "*fu* lion" to match the vase. The quartz shows feathering. Era of Ch'ien-lung. Has teakwood stand.

161—OLIVE-GREEN JADE VASE WITH COVER

Height, 12¼ inches; width, 6⅝ inches.

Pilgrim bottle shape, with short neck and two carved elephant-head
handles, their trunks forming loops. Obverse and reverse with meander
bordering, enclosing five bats and a circular *shou* emblem of longevity,
which involves a small swastika (*wan-tse*) cross. The cover, with
escalloped bordering, sustains a low carved lotus-pod knob. Has teakwood stand.

162—COLLECTION OF SMALL FU LIONS

Size of case: Height, 10 inches; 14½ inches square.

Consisting of nine examples, mounted on a stand and under a glass case: Carnelian agate group of lions at play; recumbent lion carved in rare turquoise; amethyst lion with cub and small sphere; red amber lion, recumbent; black and white jade lion, recumbent; pure white jade lion and two cubs; crystal lion, recumbent; carnelian agate lion, recumbent; lapis-lazuli lion, recumbent.

163—CRYSTAL APPLIQUÉ VASE

Height, 8½ inches; diameter, 5½ inches.

Pyriform with slightly flattened section and angular handles. The *pietra-dura* incrustations in floral and bird motifs include varied nephrite, jadeite, carnelian-agate, lapis-lazuli, amber, amethyst, boneite, coral and aventurine or "gold stone." A unique example, bearing an openwork boneite panel underneath, of geometrical pattern, under which the Imperial mark apepars. Era of Ch'ien-lung (1736-1795). Has teakwood stand.

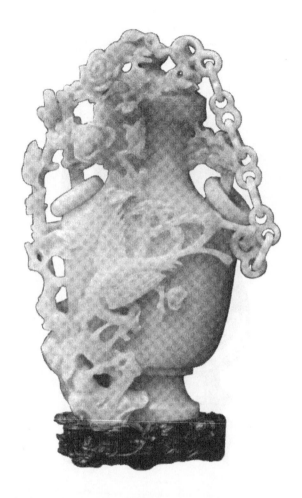

164—PURE-WHITE JADE VASE WITH COVER AND CHAIN

Height, 11¾ inches; width, 7 inches.

Flat ovated shape with dragon-head handles and loose rings, one of the handles holding the jade chain that is attached to the cover. The raised embellishment on the obverse presents the fabled phoenix on a rocky ledge, sculptured in bold relief and flanked by a flowering tree which extends to the upper rim. Reverse displays a bird and floral spray carved in low relief. Dome-shaped cover, carved with an open blossom and a loop holding the linked chain. Fashioned from one mass of limpid white nephrite of suet-like translucent quality. Ta Ch'ing Dynasty. Has teakwood stand.

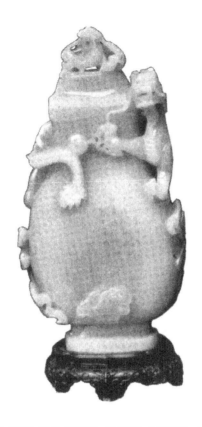

165—*WHITE JADE DRAGON VASE WITH COVER*

Height, 11½ inches; width, 6 inches.

Flattened shape with oviform contour; the sculptured embellishment including a large dragon which encircles the neck in quest of the omnipotent jewel, rendered in relief with openwork and undercutting. A smaller dragon appears below near the base. Obverse includes an inscription in four lines, copied from Emperor Ch'ien-lung's "Instruction for Parents," and the reverse shows symbolical cloud scrolls. The cover presents a large coiled dragon knob. Date: Era of Ch'ien-lung (1736-1795). Has teakwood stand.

166—OLIVE-GREEN JADE LEAF TRAY

Length, 12½ inches; width, 7½ inches.

Fashioned in natural form of a large repand leaf, from green (*pai-yü*) nephrite, the details including a cicada, and veining on either side, together with a foot stalk bearing a small prickled fruit. XVIIIth century. Has elaborately carved teakwood stand.

167—LARGE GREEN JADE JU-I, OR SCEPTER

Length, 20 inches.

Slender curved wand in conventional form fashioned from one piece of moss-green jade, supplemented by three white jade plaquettes. The head-piece is ornamented with an elephant carrying a vase, attended by a youth who carries a sacred *ling-chi* or polypary. On the center panel are two boys with a flower vase, and the lower plaquette is invested with the *yang* and *yin* emblems and wave motifs. Has green cord and red tassel pendant. Era Ch'ien-lung (1736-1795).

(Illustrated.)

168—ROCK-CRYSTAL GROUP

Height, 9½ inches; width, 9 inches.

Representing the philosopher Lao-Tsze, with a peach, his staff and a gourd, accompanied by a deer, freely posed next to a square jar, the cover of which is surmounted by a boy with a bat emblem. The reverse of the vase has a simple relief carving presenting fungus growths and a flying bat. Flawless material with perfect lapidary finish. Teakwood stand.

169—WHITE JADE JU-I, OR SCEPTER

Length, 17¾ inches.

In the conventional form, with gracefully undulating stem and a broad, scrolled leaf-medallion head. The head is carved in bold relief with a seated figure and Buddhistic symbol; the foot with an elephant and symbols in low relief. Entire rim of head and stem and both upper and lower surfaces of the stem, or handle, covered with gilt inscription. The whole carved from one piece of translucent bluish-white jade.

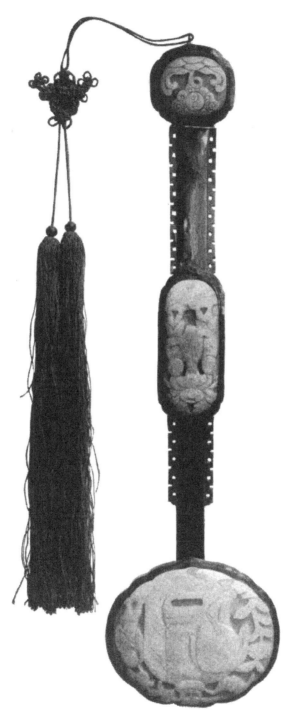

167

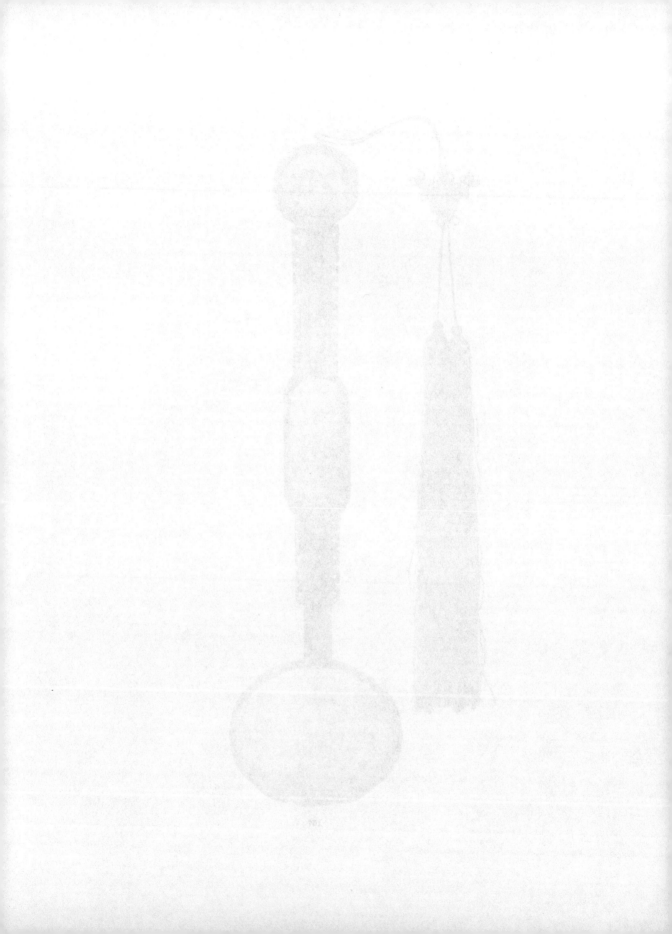

170—LARGE WHITE JADE BEAKER

Height, 10¼ inches; width, 6⅝ inches.

Flattened rectangular form, with spreading neck, and sustaining two bird-like heads on the shoulder with undercutting and loose suspended rings, the white nephrite showing a light sea-green tint with translucency. The form copied after an ancient bronze. Deep sunken foot which bears the Imperial Ch'ien-lung mark, as specially made for the palace. Has teakwood stand.

171—TWO QUADRANGULAR JADEITE VASES WITH COVERS

Height, 13 inches; width, 3 inches.

Fashioned with their covers from white jadeite showing emerald-green clouding and translucent quality. The delicately incised embellishment on the four sides, uniformly displaying a *lei-wên* meander or angular "thunder-scroll" bordering, encloses circular dragon crests and square *shou* character panels. Dome-shaped covers with boldly raised foliated carving, including four loops and loose rings. Bear Imperial marks. Era of Ch'ien-lung (1736-1795). Ta Ch'ing Dynasty. Have teakwood stands.

172—UNIQUE LARGE CARVED JADEITE PLATE

Diameter, 12½ inches.

Presenting a rare blended white *fei-ts'ui* of typical translucent quality, with slight greenish flecking and yellow veining. Inner surface carved in low relief with a peony-tree motif, the branches bearing large flowers and foliage. Date: XVIIIth century. Ta Ch'ing Dynasty. Has upright teakwood stand with jade inset.

173—TALL ROCK-CRYSTAL VASE WITH COVER

Height, 12¾ inches; width, 6 inches.

Flattened rectangular form with rounded contour and receding neck, and two dragon-head handles and loose rings. Obverse and reverse simply polished. Interior deeply hollowed and polished uniformly with the exterior. Cover of oblong shape, with slanting sides and knob and without ornament. The material is flawless and shows great brilliancy. Ta Ch'ing Dynasty. Teakwood stand.

174—LIGHT SEA-GREEN JADE VASE WITH APPLIED ORNAMENT

Height, 9⅝ inches; width, 5 inches.

Graceful flattened shape with oviform contour and attenuated neck, sustaining two small angular handles. The *pietra-dura* embellishment, in variously colored jades, lapis-lazuli, carnelian agate, turquoise and coral, appliqué, present pine and plum trees, blossoms, cranes and birds, together with fungus clumps. On the neck are orchid flowers in like hard stone incrustation. Ta Ch'ing Dynasty. Has teakwood stand.

175—WHITE JADE BRUSH HOLDER

Height, 6¼ inches; diameter, 6 inches.

Cylindrical and massive form in rare white jade, showing a suet-like translucency, strongly marked with a yellowish zone on one side. Carved in bold relief with a panoramic landscape subject, rendered with deep undercutting, displaying mountain and lake scenery, together with pine trees, ravines and cliffs. A poetic inscription in gilt characters, copied from an essay on "The Seasons," by the Emperor Ch'ien-lung, appears on one side of the exterior. Underneath there is an incised seal mark (indicating an imperial object specially made for the palace) in four characters. Ch'ien-lung era. Ta Ch'ing Dynasty.

Interior fitted with yellow silk panel, holding four implements, viz: (*A*) White jade *ju-i* (scepter) incrusted with varied hard stones. (*B*) Two jade brushes, with carved handles. (*C*) The *tai ping ch'e* (used for massage purposes) has a green jade handle with agate, quartz and aventurine (gold stone) rollers. Fitted on dragon-headed form and intersected by rare sulphur-yellow jade rundles.

(*Illustrated.*)

176—LARGE WHITE AND GREEN JU-I, OR SCEPTER

Length, 17¾ inches.

The handle, fashioned in conventional form, of dark green jade, is surmounted by a white jade head-piece, the latter carved in low relief with the characters *shuang-hsi* or "wedded joy," usually inscribed on wedding presents, surrounded by the Buddhistic (*Pa chi-hsiang*) emblems of happy augury. The carved handle has similar emblems and a *shou* character of longevity. Date: XVIIIth century.

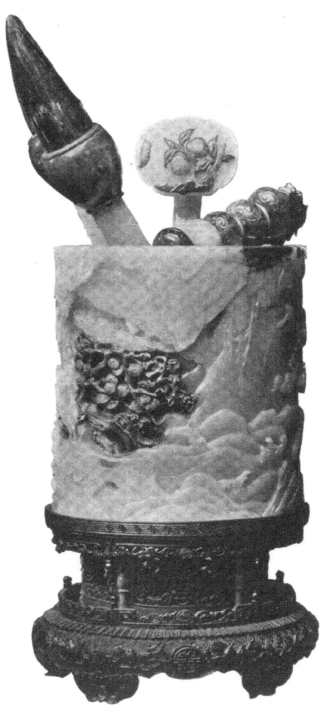

177—WHITE JADE TRIPOD INCENSE BOWL WITH COVER

Height, 9⅜ inches; diameter, 7½ inches.

Low round shape with flanged neck and two dragon-head handles, including openwork carving with loose rings. The body, raised on three monster-head feet, is without other ornament, and shows translucent and even quality enhanced by fine polishing. Dome-shaped cover of like material sustaining a large grotesque free standing "*fu* lion" and a smaller one looking up at it. Foot underneath bears an Imperial mark: "Specially made, era of Ch'ien-lung" (1736-1795). Has teakwood stand.

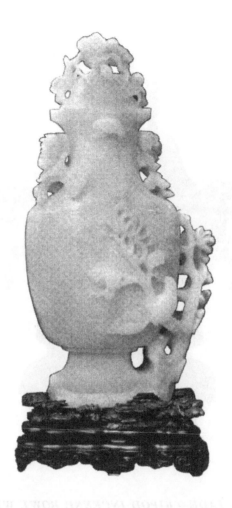

178—LARGE WHITE JADE VASE WITH COVER

Height, 13 inches; diameter, 6½ inches.

Graceful ovated shape; sculptured in pure white nephrite of suet-like translucency, and of the variety commonly called "mutton fat" jade, with open floral handles. On the obverse a phœnix and a blossoming tree, beautifully rendered in free relief, with delicate openwork and rounded undercutting. Reverse showing two small birds and tree boughs. The cover of like material is crowned with clustering blossoms in free relief. Imposing example of the XVIIIth century. Ta Ch'ing Dynasty. Has double stand of carved ivory and teakwood.

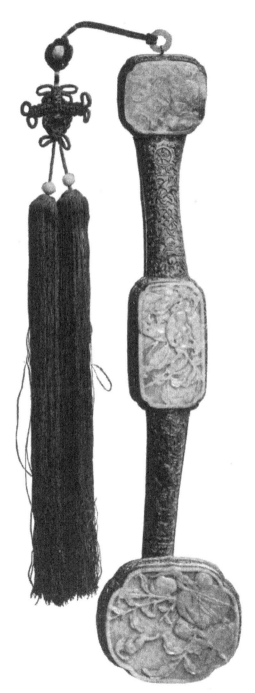

182

179—GREENISH WHITE JADE FUNGUS VASE

Height, 7 inches; width, 10 inches.

Sculptured in natural form of a large branching polypary, or the sacred *ling-chih*, deeply hollowed out and turned upright midst stems and smaller *ling-chih* clumps, with openwork and undercutting. Bears Imperial studio mark: "Made era of Ch'ien-lung." Has teakwood stand.

180—MOSS-GREEN JADEITE PLATE

Diameter, 10⅞ inches.

Deep shape without ornament; beautifully polished to bring out the deep moss-like flecking and grayish-white tones suggesting a dark variety, poetically termed *hua hsuch tai tsao* or "moss entangled with melting snow." Ta Ch'ing Dynasty. Has carved teakwood stand.

181—ROCK-CRYSTAL VASE GROUP WITH BOY AND ELEPHANT

Height, 11½ inches; width, 8½ inches.

Fashioned in ovoid form with flattened section; the vase, including the elephant-head handles and loose rings, is flanked on one side by a small elephant, and on the other by a figure of a boy, sculptured in free relief. The body of the vessel presents a peach tree in bold relief, with openwork and undercut carving; the reverse sustaining the symbolical Buddha's-hand citron in low relief. Cover surmounted by a phœnix bird. Teakwood stand.

182—PAIR LARGE GILT BRONZE AND JADEITE SCEPTERS

Length, 20 inches.

Conventional curved wand of gilt-bronze, ornamented with the eight Buddhistic (*Pa chi-hsiang*) emblems of happy augury, and scrolls. The middle and upper and lower ends bear light emerald-green jadeite plaques, inserted with relief carving presenting the symbolic "fruits of the abundances," and allegorical bats. Reverse of handle enriched with a complicated diaper pattern, involving small swastika emblems. End ring holding red silk tassel and beaded cords. Ta Ch'ing Dynasty. On carved teakwood stand with glass case.

(Illustrated.)

183—GREENISH-WHITE JADE VASE WITH COVER

Height, 12½ inches; width, 6¼ inches.

Flattened rectangular shape with tapering contour and attenuated neck, sustaining two monster-head handles with loops and suspended rings. The carving in low relief presents a series of bands including small fungus scrolls with the *t'ao t'ieh* lineaments of the gluttonous tiger. The oblong cover is surmounted by a recumbent elephant. Vase bears incised Ch'ien-lung mark, in gold, on upper side of base. Has teakwood stand.

184—LARGE GREEN JADEITE VASE WITH COVER

Height, 13¼ inches; width, 6¼ inches.

Graceful ovated form, with receding neck sustaining two boldly carved dragon-head handles, with loose rings. Surrounded by a carved band of hieratic designs. The remaining surface left plain with fine polishing shows varied tones of green and is slightly marked by black veining. Dome-shaped cover with similar band of archaic carving, surmounted by a lion, freely carved with the usual emblematic sphere. Date: XVIIIth century. Has teakwood stand.

185—LARGE SEA-GREEN CELADON JAR WITH COVER

Height, 12¼ inches; diameter, 7½ inches.

Fashioned in so-called gallipot form, without ornamentation, the highly polished nephrite presenting a light céladon color, with interesting clouding of gray tones on one side. Cover of like material, presenting upturned scalloped rim and knob finial. Panel underneath with mark of the Ch'ien-lung period; made for the Imperial palace. Has teakwood stand carved in form of thalamus.

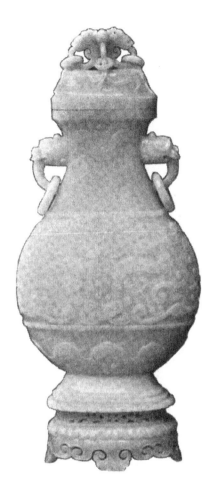

186—*LARGE WHITE JADE VASE WITH COVER AND STAND*

Total height, 21 inches; width, 14 inches.

Tall flattened oviform, with attenuated neck sustaining two monster-head handles with loose rings. Body carved elaborately with serpentine bordering and archaic scroll motifs, in low relief, together with dragon-head serpents and bosses, copied from ancient bronzes. The dome-shaped cover sustaining four monster heads looped with loose rings. The white jade stand fashioned in conventional form with open-work carving. Foot underneath bears Ch'ien-lung mark: specially made for the palace. Ta Ch'ing Dynasty.

187—DARK-GREEN JADE VASE WITH COVER AND STAND

Height, 21½ inches; width, 14 inches.

Tall flattened oviform, with attenuated neck supporting two
monster-head handles with loops and loose rings. Body surrounded
by archaic scroll motifs carved in low relief, involving *haou teen* or
admonitory ogre lineaments, copied from ancient bronzes. The neck
is encircled by a lanceolated bordering followed by a raised band with
bosses, which is repeated below, while fretted meanders finish upper
and lower rims. Bears gilt inscription on the neck, a copy of a poem
by the Emperor Ch'ien-lung, written to a friend. The dome-shaped
cover sustains four monster-head loops, with free rings. Has olive-
green jade stand in conventional form, with delicate pierced carving.
Imperial mark underneath: Specially made. Era of Ch'ien-lung.

194

188—LARGE ROCK-CRYSTAL VASE WITH COVER

Height, 14½ inches; width, 7 inches.

Flattened rectangular form, with rounded contour and contracted neck supporting two dragon-head handles with free rings. Bold carving all around the body, showing a deer with a flying crane and a pine tree. The three emblematical "fruits of the abundances" beautifully rendered with deep undercutting. Domed cover, carved with bat and cloud motif, sustaining a large truncated knob. Rare example of clear rock crystal, its flawless quality showing brilliant under the fine polishing. Ta Ch'ing Dynasty. Teakwood stand.

189—OLIVE-GREEN JADE RUSTIC VASE

Height, 13½ inches; width, 7¾ inches.

Fashioned in tall rustic form of the sacred *ling-chih* or fungus-clumps, strongly rendered and intermingled with the allegorical five bats, signifying as many blessings, while the fungi mean long life. Bears incised Imperial mark of four characters. Era of Ch'ien-lung. Has teakwood stand.

190—LARGE ROCK-CRYSTAL VASE WITH COVER

Height, 15⅛ inches; width, 6 inches.

Rectangular form with receding neck supporting two dragon-head handles and loose rings. Obverse and reverse presenting the symbolical "triangle" or "sounding stone" (*ch'ing*) with fillets, flanked by scrolling bands, which reach to the narrow sections and form loops. Dome-shaped cover surmounted by grotesque dragon. Teakwood stand.

191—DARK-GREEN JADE MOUNTAIN

Height, 12¾ inches; width, 7 inches.

A carving in olive-green nephrite (*pai-yü*) to represent a high mountain peak, with figures of a sage living in retreat and visitors, pine trees, a cascade, a pavilion, a brook and a bridge, in openwork and undercutting; reverse representing cliffs, trees and a stream. Ta Ch'ing Dynasty.

192—LARGE LAPIS-LAZULI TABLE SCREEN

Height, 11 inches; with stand, 21 inches; width, 14 inches.

Oblong upright panel of deep blue Eastern lapis, sculptured with a mountainous landscape subject, including human figures, trees, ledges, bridges and cloud strata. A pavilion appears above on the cliffs, being the mountain retreat of a scholar. Reverse, without ornament, simply polished. In teakwood stand.

197

197A

193—LARGE ROCK-CRYSTAL VASE WITH COVER AND FIGURES

Height, 14¼ inches; width, 6 inches.

Fashioned in beaker form; the spreading neck sustaining monster-head handles with loose rings, while the base is flanked on two sides by the figures of boys bearing emblems. Neck and base uniformly presenting a serrated leaf bordering in archoic form. Cover, with leaf bordering in corresponding form, supports fungiform handles which hold free suspended rings, and two more rings are on top combined with the fungiform finial. Teakwood stand.

194—PAIR OF JADE PAGODA SHRINE COLUMNS

Total height, 30 inches; width at base, 9 inches.

Tibetan stupa-like form (*fo-ta*), fashioned in a combination of green and white nephrite, with openwork carving, and including a series of eight small green jade figures which are posed on the sloping shoulder of the lower divisions, the remaining ornament comprehending Buddhistic emblems and *shou* or longevity characters. Each column contains within the pierced lower division, and seen through an aperture of ovoid form as a frame, a small gold-plated image of Avalōkitês-vara, Goddess of Mercy; and the tapering cone-shaped upper section, resting within a white jadeite railing, shows a series of grayish-green jade openwork rings.

The top, with a dome-like umbrella of white jadeite having a coral beaded fringe, is crowned by a gourd of jade with gilt fillets, bearing an amethyst crescent, a turquoise ball and a coral "*lun*" emblem enveloped in flames, like a monstrance. Carved and green-stained ivory base, with a separate gilt bronze and champlevé enameled stand. Ta Ch'ing Dynasty.

(*Illustrated.*)

NOTE: The above columns appear to be miniatures of a stupa or tower erected at Yan Chou, on the Imperial Canal.

195—LARGE NEW YEAR PALACE TABLET

Height, 28 inches; width, 14 inches.

Double-gourd shape, of carved teakwood with gilt fretting and an elaborate gilt bronze mounting, including two medallions that enclose felicitous characters (*Ta Chi*) meaning "great good luck." The remaining surfaces sustain Buddhistic emblems of happy augury, with five bats, to suggest as many blessings. The sides hold long fish handles of gilt bronze, cast with cord and tassel mountings. Teakwood stand.

Presenting a pink lacquered ground, with incrusted semi-precious stones fashioned into human and floral forms, in characteristic eighteenth century design. Subject with garden terrace showing Si Wang Mu, the Taoist Queen Mother of the West, accompanied by fairies of her court. Emblematic fruits are represented in various vases and graceful baskets. Teakwood frame.

196a—*LARGE PIETRA-DURA PICTURE PANEL*

Height, 32 inches; width, 46 inches.

Pendant to foregoing. Presenting similar pink lacquered ground with incrusted jade and semi-precious stones, including flower vases and symbolical fruit, together with the immortal philosopher, Lao-Tsze, an attendant and a deer. Date: XVIIIth century. Teakwood frame.

197—*LARGE PICTURE SCREEN WITH TEAKWOOD MOUNT-ING*

Height, 46½ inches; width, 49 inches.

Oblong panel, with blue lacquered ground enriched by varied forms of wall vases executed in enamel painting on copper and in other materials, the other objects showing plants, scholar's emblems, a chess board, bundle of books, musical instruments, treasured vessels and a basket with pomegranates, executed in various semi-precious stones and coral. Date: XVIIIth century.

(Illustrated.)

197A—*LARGE PICTURE SCREEN* (*Companion to preceding*)

Height, 42 inches; width, 49 inches.

Oblong panel with red lacquered ground and applications of vases, plants and emblematical devices in wall-vase form, executed in Peking enamel on copper, colored ivories being utilized for the floral forms. Included with the above appear small gilt bronze plaquettes.

(*Illustrated.*)

198—*LAPIS-LAZULI TEMPLE SET*

Consisting of five pieces, fashioned from homogeneous Eastern lapis-lazuli of azure-blue tone. Mounted in parcel-gilt bronze, the carved embellishment enriched with incrustations 'of semi-precious stones in floral and scroll designs, in part composed of carnelian agate, turquoise and amethyst.

A: *The Incense Burner* fashioned in quadrangular shape of an ancient sacrificial vessel (*ting*), raised on four feet. The body, with vertical dentated ridges at the corners and including two angular rim handles, sustains inlaid lotus flower motifs inlaid with varied semi-precious stones. The cover, of like material, is surmounted by a rose quartz knob. With massive teakwood stand.

Height, 16¼ inches; width, 10 inches.

B: *Two Beakers in Quadrangular Form.* Matching the preceding.

Height, 13 inches; width, 5 inches.

C: *Two Pricket Candlesticks.* Including a carved carnelian-agate, in tubular form, with a gilt bronze dragon mounting midst cloud scrolls, topped by a plain agate emblem. Early XVIIIth century.

Height, 24 inches; width, 5½ inches.

(*Illustrated.*)

199—TWO GRAND CIRCULAR TABLE SCREENS WITH JADE APPLICATIONS

Height, complete, 89 inches; width of table, 42 inches; diameter of panel, 33 inches.

Mounted upon tall table stands. The large circular picture panels within carved teakwood framing present a yellowish lacquered ground relieved by numerous carved jade insertions in the form of treasured objects and emblems, including vases holding symbolical flowers, sacrificial-vessel forms, libation cups used in ancient times to hold the elixir of life, images of horses, and treasured books and elephants with treasure vases. The varied fruits symbolize the three abundances, and there are also boats of pleasure, with fish dragons to suggest advancement in rank. Date: XVIIIth century.

(*Illustrated.*)

199

199

IMPERIAL ENTRANCE TO PRINCE KUNG'S PALACE

SECOND AFTERNOON'S SALE

FRIDAY, FEBRUARY 28, 1913

AT THE AMERICAN ART GALLERIES

BEGINNING AT 2.30 O'CLOCK

200—*MINIATURE CARVED IVORY DOUBLE-GOURD AND CHAIN ORNAMENT*

Height of gourd, 3½ inches; total length, with chain, 31 inches.

The gourd-form carved with reticulated fret border and low-relief bat motifs in movable but not detachable sections, the stopper holding a delicate chain of carved ivory, with tiny bells, baskets and gourds as pendants; carved from one ivory piece, the stopper being held within the larger gourd.

201—*MINIATURE CARVED IVORY DOUBLE-GOURD ORNA-MENT WITH CHAIN*

Height of gourd, 3⅝ inches; length, with chain, 17 inches.

Carved with reticulated borders and intricate bat and cloud forms in low relief, the stopper holding a delicate ivory linked chain with pendants, carved from one piece and held within the gourd. Similar to preceding.

202—*MINIATURE IVORY DRAGON BARGE*

Height, 4¾ inches; length, 5¾ inches.
Height, with stand, 6½ inches.

Delicately carved to represent an Imperial pleasure boat in miniature, the head of a dragon forming the figure-head. Deck built with a two-story structure resembling a garden pavilion, showing an open grilled interior with view of the Emperor's chair in each stateroom. Accessories include delicate fretwork and railing and an Imperial pendant flying on the staff. Double stand of ivory and teakwood.

203—MINIATURE IVORY PHŒNIX BARGE

Height, 4¾ inches; length, 6 inches.
Height, with stand, 6¼ inches.

Companion to preceding. Delicately carved to represent a *fêng* or phœnix barge in miniature. The deck, built with a two-story structure to resemble a garden pavilion, shows an interior with empty chairs for the Empress's use. Accessories include delicate fretwork and railing, and an Imperial pennant on its staff.

204—SOLID CARVED IVORY HAND-REST

Length, 9 by 2⅜ inches.

Under side with sunken carving, delicately rendered in free relief, presenting a mountainous landscape with eight Taoist immortals riding upon varied fabled animals to the place of meeting. Lao-Tsze is seen on his stork, flying toward those below. Showing marvelous execution in undercutting and free relief. The curved upper surface with inscription signed by Te Yuen. Ta Ch'ing Dynasty.

205—SOLID CARVED IVORY HAND-REST

Length, 9½ by 2⅜ inches.

Similar to preceding. The obverse side with sunken decoration, showing fragmentary landscape, including pavilion, lake and boatmen. Underside presenting more elaborate landscape carving, together with a coterie of scholars assembled in a pine grove, beautifully rendered with delicate undercutting. Ta Ch'ing Dynasty.

206—CARVED IVORY HAND-REST

Length, 9¾ inches; width, 2¾ inches.

Similar to the preceding, with plain obverse side; underside carved with elaborate landscape subject, including figures of sages or immortals, within pavilions, or crossing upon a bridge, while others appear riding in the sea on the backs of fabled animals. Ta Ch'ing Dynasty.

207—PAIR OF CARVED IVORY VASES

Height, 5⅛ inches; diameter, 3½ inches.

Cylindrical form, with panoramic landscape subjects and human figures beautifully carved in bold relief, with undercutting, and showing most minute details. One vase represents an assemblage of Taoist Immortals riding upon fabled animals to their place of meeting; the queen fairy, Si Wang Mu, appearing above on her fabled paradise bird. The pendant vase shows another panoramic landscape, delicately carved, with immortals and deities in free relief, including Shou Lao, the god of longevity, and the goddess of mercy, Kuan-yin, riding on an elephant, while another immortal rides heavenward upon a dragon.

208—CARVED IVORY HANGING VASE WITH STANDARD OF TEAKWOOD

Height, with standard, 13 inches; width, 7½ inches.

Graceful form with flaring rim, representing the basket of Lan Ts'ai-ho, a female Rishi or Taoist fairy, delicately rendered in open-work with linked chain and hanger. The reticulation and carved decoration consists of emblematical fruit and butterflies, with border motifs. Ta Ch'ing Dynasty.

209—RHINOCEROS-HORN CUP

Height, 4½ inches; length, 10¼ inches.

Fashioned in shape of a boat with long prow, the upper part of the stern section carved with the figure of a sage seated before a bower of symbolical flowers. Openwork carving of fruits and foliations. On one side a felicitous inscription. Date: XVIIth century.

210—CARVED RHINOCEROS-HORN CUP

Height, 5½ inches; width, 7 by 4½ inches.

Conventional form of libation cup; the sculptured work presenting a landscape with pine trees, pavilion, and numerous figures of sages or scholars occupied in social discourse over their tea and books. Date: XVIIth century. Ming Dynasty. Teakwood stand.

211—CARVED RHINOCEROS-HORN CUP

Height, 6 inches; diameter, 7¼ inches.

Embellished with an openwork landscape and figure subject representing a garden scene with groups of scholars seated at a table, and an approaching horseman followed by a boy with a wheelbarrow. The accessories include a pavilion occupied by a sage, and pine trees with pierced work in the open rendering of the branches. Bears an inscription on one side. Ming Dynasty.

COLLECTION OF TOMB JADES

212—GRAYISH-GREEN AND BLACK JADE AMULET

Length, 3 inches.

Representing a recumbent tiger, or *p'i-sieh* emblem, in so-called tomb jade. Carved teakwood stand.

213—JADE GOAT GROUP

Height, 3 inches; length, 3½ inches.

Representing a large goat lying down, with a smaller goat at his side and another on his back. On his flank the *yang* and *yin* symbols. White nephrite with drab tones and black clouding. Has teakwood stand.

214—ORIENTAL AGATE PAPER WEIGHT

Height, 2 inches; length, 3½ inches.

In the form of a recumbent tiger, showing interesting gray and brown conglomerate structure. Early XVIIIth century. Has teakwood stand.

215—JADE WATER COUPE

Length, 4½ inches; width, 3½ inches.

In form of a recumbent duck, flattened and hollowed for a writer's water vessel. Light céladon-toned nephrite, showing russet-red clouding. Han Dynasty. Teakwood stand.

216—JADE UNICORN

Height, 3 inches; length, 4½ inches.

Representing the quadruped in recumbent position with legs directly under the body. Céladon-colored nephrite with russet zones. A so-called tomb jade. Han Dynasty. Teakwood stand.

217—WHITE AGATE FU LION

Height, 2¼ inches; width, 5 inches.

In recumbent form, resting upon a rock, the grotesque and vigorously carved animal showing translucent gray and yellowish tones. Carved in one piece with its stand.

218—RED AND WHITE JADE COUPE

Height, 1½ inches; width, 4¼ inches.

Shallow oblong form with indented corners, plainly fashioned from an old nephrite boulder, showing yellowish-red clouding, from iron rust. Date, probably Ming. Has teakwood stand.

219—DARK STEATITE INK PALLET

Length, 5 inches; width, 3¼ inches.

Shallow form, surrounded on one side by a lizard-like dragon, with bifurcated tail. Dark olive stone with lighter blendings. Bears Imperial seal mark of the era of Ch'ien-lung (1736-1795). Teakwood stand.

220—ORIENTAL YELLOW AGATE SEAL

Height, 3½ inches; width, 3½ inches.

In form of a mountain, including carving in the form of pine trees, a pavilion and the figure of a sage, with an inscription with the name of the maker: Tong shou yu moo. The seal has not been deciphered; probably used by a literary personage.

221—YELLOW AGATE SMALL MOUNTAIN

Height, 5½ inches; width, 3½ inches.

Fashioned in the so-called amber-agate (*wŏng lur*), also termed *o-lo*, to represent one of the mountain retreats of a scholar. The carving on the obverse includes sheep, a pine tree, a stream, and the sun disk midst cloud forms, beautifully rendered in low relief. Reverse with simple cliffs, and including pine tree carving.

222—HAN YU JADE EMBLEM

Diameter, 3¼ inches.

In annular form, the exterior presenting a series of (*pa kua*) broken bands or divisions, in sunken form, with small boss-like studdings to represent millet grains. Used in the worship of the earth or feminine Deity Earth. Dark nephrite with green and brown zones, showing calcination and earthy incrustations. Han Dynasty.

223—WHITE JADE DAGGER

Length, 8⅛ inches.

Unique example, presenting a single-edged blade, its sides ornamented along the top with a *lei-wên* or angular "thunder scroll" border and the back with carved projections. Handle carved with openwork to represent a dragon in archaic form. Probably served as an emblem of power, or for some ceremonial purpose. Probably Ming. Date uncertain. Mounted on teakwood standard.

224—HAN YU DISK

Diameter, 4 inches.
Height, with stand, 9½ inches.

Obverse and reverse presenting the so-called "grain pattern" (*ku-pi*), small millet-like bossing in symmetrical arrangement. Grayish-white nephrite, with yellow markings. Han Dynasty. Teakwood stand.

225—SMALL COLLECTION OF TOMB JADES

Dimension of case, 7½ inches.

Consisting of ten varied symbols and pendants, including disks, rings, girdle pendants and jar-shaped amulets. Mounted on silk stands, in a square teakwood case with carved cover.

226—HAN YU DISK

Diameter, 5½ inches; total height, 8½ inches.

Obverse and reverse uniformly presenting small convoluted cloud scrolls. Red nephrite, showing light greenish tones. Used in the worship of the Deity of Heaven. Han Dynasty. Mounted on teakwood stand.

227—JADE CEREMONIAL TABLET

Height, 10 inches; width, 3¾ inches.

Typical form of a flattened obelisk crossed by a circular band, used in worship in connection with the sun, moon, planets and constellations. Cut from one piece of ancient nephrite, the circular division embellished with a dragon scroll, and the vertical column with an ancient planetary device, at the top, while the three pointed rocks of the "dragon gate" appear below. Reverse carries an incised inscription. Sung Dynasty.

228—LARGE HAN YU DISK

Diameter, 5¼ inches.
Height, with stand, 8¾ inches.

Dark nephrite showing russet-red and grayish céladon intermingled with brown tones. Without decoration, and presenting a shagreen surface. Han Dynasty. Teakwood stand.

229—HAN YU JADE TABLET

Height, 8½ inches.

In ancient vertical or flattened obelisk form, fashioned in grayish-white nephrite with green, yellow and brownish clouding. Presenting the twelve symbols, or *Chang* ornaments, referred to in classical history as "emblems of the ancients," and illustrated by commentators of the Sung Dynasty. Such emblems were embroidered on the Imperial robes, and in lesser number were restricted to princes and nobles. Reverse sustains two engraved marks of ancient lore. Teakwood stand.

230—ANCIENT STEATITE INK SLAB

Length, 8 inches.

Fashioned in flat oval form, suggesting a fruit, with a dragon carved at one end and a young dragon at either side, with serpentine bodies and cleft tails. Small elliptical hollow for the water. Gray, olive-green and yellowish tones. Date uncertain.

231—HAN YU JADE TUBE

Height, 6⅛ inches; width, 3 inches.

Plain quadrangular shape with hexagonal neck and base. Hollow tubular interior. A form used in ceremonies of worship in connection with the earth or one-quarter thereof. Grayish-green nephrite shows rich russet-red clouding. Han Dynasty.

232—HAN YU JADE RING SYMBOL

Exterior diameter, 4¾ inches.

Massive annular form, with carved embellishment on the exterior presenting a pair of *shih-lung* dragons amidst cloud patches, in quest of the flaming jewel. Dark nephrite with russet-red, brown and céladon-colored zones. While probably used for some ritual in the past, it may also have served as a token of respect from feudal princes. Han Dynasty. Mounted on silk-covered base of teakwood.

233—HAN YU RING SYMBOL

Diameter, 6½ inches; height, with stand, 12 inches.

Flattened annular form, of the prescribed dimensions, the carved embellishment on the two faces presenting tiger-mask lineaments in sunken and outline carving. A princely token of respect, and also formerly used for sacrificial or religious ceremonies. Dark blended nephrite presenting russet-red, olive-green and grayish zones. Han Dynasty. Mounted upon stand.

234—*HAN YU JADE DISK SYMBOL*

Diameter, 6½ inches; total height, 10½ inches.

Obverse presenting a pair of *shih-lung* dragons with cleft tails and scrolling forms, in low relief; the reverse showing four *pa kua* emblems alternately with four *yang-ying* devices, cut in low relief and finished by a meander border at the edge. Dark blended nephrite showing brown and grayish zones. Han Dynasty. In teakwood standard.

Fashioned of dark olive-green *hua-shi*, or steatite, of a rare variety, decorated with the writings of famed scholars. Consisting of nine objects, viz.:

Small table screen with an oblong panel showing a landscape subject, with the inscription, "High mountains, more clouds"; made by Yê Chu. Reverse with a stanza in ancient style, copied from a writer of the T'ang Dynasty.

Ink slab with cover, bearing an inscription copied from Yê Chu, with a studio mark.

Small brush cylinder, with the same seal, and including an inscription of good wishes from the famed writing by Wong Shê Gê, one of the great scholars of the past.

Quadrangular vase bearing a seal and inscriptions copied from four noted scholars.

Oval water receptacle with an inscription.

Oblong hand or brush rest, with inscription meaning, "May your son and grandson live long and prosper," copied by Yê Chu.

Brush rest, representing the five famed mountains and bearing studio seal of the maker and a copy of a queen's seal.

Round color box, bearing inscription: "Yê Chu studio made."

Leaf-shaped tray, carved with stem and veining and having a long inscription on its inner surface.

236—*BLENDED GRAY AND BLACK JADE VASE*

Height, 8⅞ inches; diameter, 4 inches.

Oviform, with dragon and tiger mask carving in relief; shoulder and base encircled by a leaf bordering; fret band at neck. The dark grayish-white nephrite with black flecking and veining.

237—*GRAY JADE INCENSE HOLDER*

Height, 8 inches; width, 5¾ inches.

Oblong, on four curved legs with grotesque masks; upstanding rim handles. Sides decorated with archaic dragon scroll carving in low relief on a fretted ground and intersected by dentated ridges at the corners and at the centers of the sides. The decoration is concluded at the rim by a meander band. Form and ornament copied from an ancient sacrificial vessel. Date uncertain. Has teakwood cover with *han yü* mounting.

238—BROWN AND GRAYISH-WHITE JADE FIGURE

Height, 6¾ inches; width, 4½ inches.

Carved from an ancient boulder, showing weathered red and yellow-ish-brown tones, with purplish-gray clouding; the head carved in a white interior zone. Representing Yen-Tsze, one of the Chinese paragons of filial piety, his shoulders and back hidden under the hide of a stag, while he is carrying a bucket for deer's milk to be used for his mother's eyes. Date uncertain. Has teakwood stand.

239—GRAY AND BLACK FLECKED JADE VASE

Height, 6⅜ inches; diameter, 5 inches.

Flattened oviform, with contracted neck and base. Obverse and reverse presenting archaic dragon forms in low relief, with reversed heads surrounding a circular *shou* character. A narrow bordering at neck finishes the decoration. So-called *han yü* or "tomb jade." While its date is uncertain, it may be ascribed to the T'ang or one of the short preceding dynasties. Has teakwood stand.

240—GREEN JADE STATUETTE

Height, 12½ inches; width, 5½ inches.

Representing Kuan-yin (Avalōkitês-vara), the goddess of mercy, sculptured in seated position in olive-green nephrite, her right arm resting on her knee, and holding a *chao-chu* or string of beads in both hands. Ascribable to the T'ang Dynasty. Carved teakwood stand of lotus design.

241—BLACK JADE SHRINE GROUP

Height, 9¾ inches; width, 8½ inches.
Height, with stand, 13 inches.

Representing a seated deity, crudely sculptured, flanked by acolyte and a flower vase, the figures within an arched background raised on a stand. The material shows dark brown, gray and black marking. Reverse bears an inscription with date. Eastern Han. Era of King Keen Wa (25-220 A.D.). Attesting seal of Ye Yen Gu Yen, made by his student, Chang Gen Jei. Mounted on a carved teakwood stand, which is surrounded with inscriptions.

242—GREEN SOAPSTONE LION GROUP

Height, 7½ inches; diameter, 10 inches.

Representation of the grotesque *tai shih* or "*fu* lion," guarding its young and holding the *ch'iu* (ball) emblem. Freely sculptured from an even-toned green steatite. Has open carved teakwood stand.

243—GREEN JADE TABLE SCREEN

Height, 11¼ inches; width, 5⅛ inches.
Height, with stand, 14¾ inches.

Oblong panel of upright form, showing typical "spinach-green" nephrite with a slight speckling of black. Obverse bearing graven characters with gilding in Mongolian script; the reverse plainly polished. Has teakwood stand.

244—UNIQUE JADE CELT-LIKE TABLET

Height, 11½ inches; width, 4 inches.

Large, flattened tapering form as of a broad, inverted lancehead, the lower part finished with a convoluted lanceolation, while the upper end sustains a winged Garuda figure in squatted form. Obverse and reverse include lateral ridges, called "teeth" by the Chinese. The remaining surfaces display hieratic motifs and tiger-mask lineaments, together with small convoluted cloud scrolling. Ascribable to the Ming Dynasty. Has teakwood stand.

245—HAN YU JADE TUBE

Height, 8½ inches; width, 3½ inches.

Rectangular, with rounded ring-like neck and base and hollow tubular interior. Grayish-green nephrite showing yellow and brown clouding. A form that was probably used in remote periods in the worship of the Earth. Polished without ornamentation. Han Dynasty. Has teakwood stand.

246—HAN YU JADE TUBE

Height, 11¼ inches; width, 4¼ inches.

Rectangular shape, of prescribed dimensions, with nine horizontal bands on the exterior, interrupted by a single vertical channel on each face. The attenuated neck and base are of rounded, ring-like form. Buff-toned nephrite with green and brown zones. Representing a typical ancient form used for the ceremony of Earth worship. Has teakwood stand. Han Dynasty.

247—LARGE HAN YU DISK

Diameter, 9⅞ inches; height, with stand, 17¾ inches.

Obverse and reverse uniformly carved with archaic dragon scrolls. Dark nephrite showing russet-red, brown and grayish zones, together with earthy incrustations from burial. Formerly used for religious worship. Han Dynasty. Has teakwood stand.

251

248—ANCIENT JADE MOUNTAIN

Height, 7¼ inches; width, 10½ inches.

Sculptured to present a mountain retreat, including a habitation surrounded by rugged cliffs and pine trees. Reverse showing projecting cliffs bare of vegetation and life and a grotto and stream. The buff-toned nephrite includes russet and brown tones or clouding. Has teakwood stand.

249—LARGE CIRCULAR JADE SOUNDING STONE

Diameter, 12½ inches; height, with stand, 23 inches.

Deep gray nephrite with russet-red speckling—a so-called "resonant stone," fashioned in the form of a flattened fish-dragon, rendered in bold outline. The surface shows a shagreened texture. Favorite ornament for a scholar. Mounted in elaborate teakwood stand.

250—UNIQUE WHITE STEATITE MOUNTAIN

Height, 8¼ inches; width, 15 inches.

Sculptured to represent a mountain scene with pavilions, horsemen, streams, boat and trees. The sides bear inscriptions which suggest the retreat of the "Nine Hermits" of ancient romance. Has teakwood stand.

251—REMARKABLE ANNULAR JADE INSIGNIA

Height, 12½ inches; width, 14¼ inches.
Height, with stand, 25 inches.

Pierced disk in large form (*ta pi*) surrounded on the outer edge by grotesque dragon forms in openwork carving, supported below by two Garudas (half-human and half-bird forms), vigorously executed. The inner circle, symbolizing heaven, shows archaic and hieratic ornament, combined with the tiger-mask lineaments. The embellishment is concluded above the circular open center by a small representation of the three rocks of the "dragon gate" cataract. Dark nephrite presenting a rich russet-red tone. Sui, or T'ang Dynasty. With teakwood standard, including lapis-lazuli and jade mounting.

252—WHITE JADE MOUNTAIN

Height, 7 inches; width, 14½ inches.

White nephrite boulder with slight markings, fashioned in form of a mountain peak. Obverse presenting cliffs and pine trees, and a group of five human figures sculptured in bold relief on a narrow ledge. Reverse includes bare rocky cliffs, defiles and ridges, together with an inscription in gilt characters after Li Hung Chang. Ta Ch'ing Dynasty. Has teakwood stand.

253—ANCIENT JADE SOUNDING STONE, OR CH'ANG

Height, 10 inches; width, 20 inches.
Height, with stand, 32 inches.

Flattened composite form presenting outlines of the tiger, tapir and dragon, executed in a perforated design with "thunder scrolls," the tiger well defined in low relief. Dark blended nephrite, including olive-green, russet-red and grayish tones. Suspended within a teakwood standard of regulation form. Han Dynasty.

254—DARK-GREEN JADE MOUNTAIN

Height, 15¾ inches; width, 14½ inches.

Fashioned from a large nephrite boulder to represent one of the five famed mountain peaks of China. The deep olive-colored, massive and smoothly polished perpendicular cliff bears poetical inscriptions lightly engraved, from essays composed by the Emperor Ch'ien-lung, and copied direct. The date and the Imperial and other seals are included. Has teakwood stand.

(Illustrated.)

The extract from Ch'ien-lung's essays is as follows:

The names of the "Five Mountains" appear in the classic poetry "Shi-Kyo," and the real sketches of them have been found in the Household Book of the Emperor Bu of the Han Dynasty, although what is mentioned about them therein is mostly without foundation, and literary men do not attach any importance to these stories.

However, such an indication only tells us how the mountains changed in appearance, turning and growing as do writings. The names are given according to the forms, but the drawn sketches do not correspond with these descriptions. In the old Geography of the Imperial Household there are several real drawings of the five mountains.

One of them was made by Du Whang, a man of the Ming Dynasty, and his work contains names of the spirits of the mountains, and their titles, powers and duties, while we fail to find any of these traditions in the official records. No doubt the men of later periods exaggerated what were mentioned in the Household books.

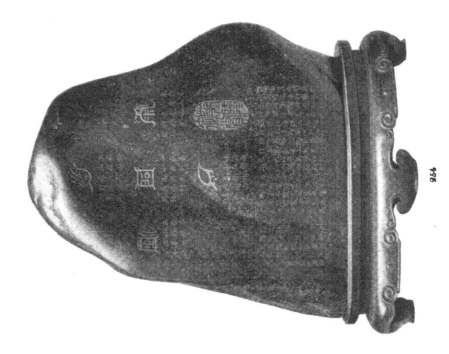

254

All things green and yellow were not like human beings, and exist subject to the natural law. What, then, can be said about the real appearance of the mountains?

In order to prove the identity of the old writings corresponding to the forms, Dong Bang Dah was appointed for the observation. As a result, it was found that the present forms agree with the old descriptions in "Ko Sheng," the book published in the Chou Dynasty, B.C.

The idea of the sketching of the mountains can be proved by "Roku-Kyo" (six classical books). It might have nobly explained itself as do the things in Yao's religion.

If we accept what Pop-Po-tze [a Chou sage] says, "Entering amidst the mountains can defend us from any dangers or evils," we will be liars.

If the five mountains were originated as were the Kuin-Ling, there must show an appearance of the root.

According to the Geography these run through the Western Extreme. Why should we limit ourselves to worship those within our boundary?

Once upon a time Hoa-Ting (a tribe of the Han period) presented us with some jades, and also great instruments for measuring high mountains, and they took the records of the five mountains in order to enrich the prosperity of our territorial resources.

Some old descriptions were not true, I mean the things mentioned in the old "Grand Geography," as, comparing again, they do not agree with each other, and I hereby correct the misinformation and express my idea on the subject.

Ch'ien-lung, 35th year,
middle of Autumn,
8th month,
Imperial Writing.

Translation of the two seals:

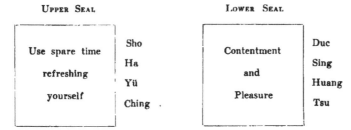

UPPER SEAL   LOWER SEAL

Use spare time   Sho   Contentment   Duc
                  Ha   Sing
refreshing   Yü   and   Huang
yourself   Ching .   Pleasure   Tsu

Of the "Five Mountains":

The Eastern mountain, named "Tai-sen,"
is situated at Tai-An-Fu (a city) in Sen-ton
province, north of Tai-on province.

The Western mountain, named "Wha-Sen,"
is situated in Sen-si province, Wha-chow
district, north of Wha-yen province.

The Southern mountain, named "Hang-Sen,"
is situated at Hang-chow-Fu (a city) in
Hue-Nan province, west of Hang-Sen province.

The Northern mountain, named "Hang-Sen," is
situated at Ta-Tung-Fu in Sen-Si province,
southeastern part of Whi-Yuen-Chow province.

EXTRAORDINARY COLLECTION OF
CHINESE BRONZES

255—ANCIENT BRONZE BEAKER

Height, 8¾ inches; diameter, 5¼ inches.

Trumpet shape, used for sacrificial wine ceremonials, middle section showing relief ornament of archaic hieratic scrolls between projecting vertical ridges. The remaining surfaces are plain and have a rich olive-brown patina speckled with yellow and green. A characteristic Chou form, attributable to the Han Dynasty. Has teakwood stand.

256—ANCIENT BRONZE SACRIFICIAL VESSEL

Height, 7¼ inches; width, 6 inches.

Oblong shape raised on four tubular feet and with two arched rim handles. The corners have vertical ridges, and an upper decorative band is enriched with archaic dragon-scrolls and small fretted groundwork. The thick incrusted patina shows malachite-green tones of rare quality. Interior bears Chou mark; Imperial seal of Wên Wang, founder of the Chou Dynasty (1169 B.C.), and has a similar green patina. Has teakwood cover and stand, the former with a jade ornament intricately carved in relief and undercutting.

257—BRONZE LIBATION VESSEL

Height, 8½ inches; width, 7 inches.

Ancient inverted helmet-shaped body, with prolonged lips, raised on three tapering feet like spear-heads and encircled by simple bands. Looped side handle. Two short stems with conical knobs rise from the rim. Rich blended brown patina with malachite-green zones. A Shang Dynasty type; probably late Chou, or Han. Similar examples figure in native books on ancient bronze. Has teakwood stand.

258—COVERED BRONZE WINE JAR

Height, 7½ inches; width, 4½ inches.

Elliptical form with bulbous body raised on low, spreading base. Archaic ornament presenting hieratic cartouches and other motifs in low relief. The interior has an ancient impressed *wan-tse* mark which is repeated on the inside of the bronze cover with slight variation. The patina shows deep olive-brown and green tones. Characteristic of the Chou Dynasty. Has teakwood stand.

259—*BRONZE SACRIFICIAL VESSEL*

Height, 8¼ inches; width, 7½ inches.

Used for fragrant wine. Molded in the shape of a dove, which carries on its back a bronze vase (*ch-iu ch'ê tsun*), and rests upon its two feet and its heavy downward-curved tail. The ornamentation is conventional and strong, and the whole is well cast. The patina with thick incrustations shows blended reddish-brown and green tones. Attributable to the Han Dynasty. A similar shape figures in the *Hsi Ch'ing Ku Ch'ien* (Catalogue of Ancient Bronzes) published under the Emperor Ch'ien-lung's direction in 1751. Has carved teakwood stand.

260—ANCIENT BRONZE TRIPOD

Height, 6 inches; width, 7½ inches.

Bulbous form, with angular upturned handles; on three curving feet without ornament. An upper rim on the body bears an incised mark of dedication, added during the Ming era. Such vessels were originally used for sacrificial food offered to ancestors. Blended russet and brown patina with verdigris-colored incrustations. Fine Han example; figured in ancient bronze catalogues. Has teakwood stand and cover, modeled after the antique.

261—INLAID BRONZE VESSEL

Height, 6½ inches; length, 7½ inches.

Molded in the hollow, standing form of a rhinoceros (*hsi*), with long ears; hinged lid on the top of the back. A collar encircling the neck is inlaid with a silver fret design, while other silver inlay is in the form of convolutions on the sides of the body, the legs and the head. Used during the Chou Dynasty to hold wine for sacrificial purposes. The olive-brown patina is blended with greenish tones. An interesting Chou form; attributable to the T'ang or Sung Dynasty. Has teakwood stand.

262—ANCIENT BRONZE BEAKER

Height, 9 inches; diameter, 5⅜ inches.

Trumpet shape. Originally used for sacrificial wine offerings, upon altars, to ancestors. Later fitted with holes for suspension. The central and lower section uniformly ornamented with fret patterns, amid which appear four small bosses. The upper section is without embellishment. Exterior and interior show a blended brown and malachite-green patina. A Chou type, figuring in ancient works on bronzes; attributable to the close of the Han era. Has teakwood stand.

263—BRONZE LIBATION TRIPOD CUP

Height, 8¾ inches; diameter, 5½ inches.

Archaic mortar-form, for sacrificial wine, with two small rim knobs and curved side handle; raised on three curved and pointed feet. The contracted center is ornamented by a dragon-scroll band of primitive form involving tiger masks. Dark olive-brown and green patina. The interior bears Chou marks. Attributable to the Han Dynasty. Has rich carved openwork stand.

264—ANCIENT BRONZE MORTAR

Height, 4¾ inches; diameter, 5¼ inches.

Massive form with simple ornamentation of a narrow incised scroll bordering, followed below by a series of elliptical protuberant bosses. The deep patina on exterior and interior is rich in russet, red, brown and malachite tones. On the foot are incised the forms of two birds. An early Chou example. Has teakwood cover, with old jade ornament carved in form of the lotus and aquatic birds, and a teakwood stand.

265—GOLD-INCRUSTED BRONZE TRIPOD VESSEL

Height, 5 inches; width, 8 inches.

Lenticular shape with vertical ridges and annulets; raised on three small figurine feet, in the form of standing bears. In the upper rim border are raised rosettes, and archaic dragon scrolls which are repeated on the lower band. Oblong panels sustain mottled brown and gold clouding. Attributable to the Sung Dynasty. Has teakwood stand and cover, the latter surmounted by jade ornament.

266—INLAID BRONZE TRIPOD VESSEL

Height, 8¼ inches; diameter, 6½ inches.

In the shape of three coalescent grotesque monster heads, presenting the tiger (*haou tëen*) lineaments, with silver damascening in combination with relief casting, and ending in three tapering feet. Low spreading neck, with rim supporting two angular handles. A rich mottled patina, showing brown and malachite-green, covers the surface. Interior bears mark (name of vessel) in Chou characters. Attributable to the Han Dynasty. Has teakwood cover with jade ornament, and teakwood stand.

267—ANCIENT BRONZE SACRIFICIAL JAR

Height, 5¼ inches; diameter, 7¾ inches.

Graceful round spreading form with two recurved monster-head handles of primitive design. The body, raised upon a low circular base, has a hieratic and serrated leaf bordering. The shoulder band, with archaic dragon scrolls and conventional tiger masks in low relief, is succeeded by a central band with hieratic motifs involving the *tao tieh* or admonitory lineaments of the gluttonous ogre. Another dragon scroll design, similar to the shoulder band but without masks, finishes the base. Rich patina, deeply incrusted, with malachite-green tones intermingled with dark purplish-blue. Interior bears a Chou mark of dedication. A similar example figures in the "Hsi Ch'ing Ku Ch'ien," published in 1751. Attributed to the Chou Dynasty. Fitted with teakwood stand.

268—BRONZE TRIPOD INCENSE BURNER

Height, 6½ inches; diameter, 5½ inches.

Of circular shape, curiously indented, the bulbous body tapering into the three feet; two upturned handles. An ornamental border below the rim bears an archaic dragon scroll with fretted groundwork of blended green and brown tones. An early form figured in native works on ancient bronze. Probably of the Han Dynasty. Has teakwood stand and cover, the latter enriched with a carved jade knob.

269—ANCIENT BRONZE BEAKER

Height, 10¼ inches; diameter, 6 inches.

Trumpet shape. Used for sacrificial wine offerings. A central ornamentated band with two vertical ridges and a series of small bosses reveals convoluted fret motifs, and similar fret designs appear on the spreading base, with bossing. Coated with a deep russet-red patina. The foot bears a Chou mark "*Mon-chu*," and hieroglyphics expressive of learning. Attributable to the Han era. Has carded teakwood stand.

270—ANCIENT BRONZE BEAKER

Height, 9 inches; diameter, 7 inches.

With wide body, flaring neck and but slightly spreading base; used for sacrificial wine ceremonials. The middle section has a relief ornamentation which involves the admonitory lineaments of the *t'ao t'ieh yên* (ogre masks), with fretted ground and vertical divisions. Neck and base are plain but present a rich blended russet-red, green and olive-brown patina. Chou type, attributable to the Han Dynasty. Has teakwood stand.

271—ANCIENT BRONZE SACRIFICIAL JAR

Height, 5 inches; diameter, 9½ inches.

Graceful rounded form with projecting animal-head handles. The neck and base bear convoluted scroll bands, interrupted by vertical ridges below and conventional tiger masks above. The bend of the body is marked by a series of uniform flutings. Rich brown and green patina. The bottom of the interior carries an inscription in sixteen characters, expressive of nobility and high ideals. Fine Chou type. Attributable to the Han Dynasty. Fitted with teakwood stand and cover, the latter mounted with a carnelian ornament.

272—REMARKABLE BRONZE SACRIFICIAL VESSEL

Height, 6½ inches; diameter, 10 inches.

Graceful round spreading form, with monster-head handles of primitive type. The body on a low base with slightly spreading foot presents relief ornament in vigorous hieratic design, with vertical ridges, involving the (*haou tëen*) lineaments of a greedy monster. Rich green and brown patina both without and within. A similar example figures in the great catalogue of bronzes printed by directions of the Emperor Ch'ien-lung in 1751. Ascribed to the Chou Dynasty. Has teakwood stand and teakwood cover with carved jade ornament.

273—ANCIENT BRONZE BOWL

Height, 5½ inches; diameter, 8 inches.

Conventional round form, with slightly flaring rim and low, spreading base. Its archaic ornament includes hieratic scrolls and the admonitory lineaments of the *t'ao t'iëh-yên* or ogre masks, with bosses and recurrent fretwork. Rim and base are finished with primitive dragon borders, with two masks appearing at the sides above. The olive-brown patina shows earthy incrustations. The interior has an ancient Chou inscription, "bright intelligence," with the name, "Quong Ming Lek." Probably late Chou. Has teakwood cover with carved jade ornament and a teakwood stand.

274—*ANCIENT BRONZE HANGING BOTTLE*

Height, 11¼ inches; diameter, 6 inches.

Cucumiform, tapering toward the curved aperture and with a circular rimmed base. One side is fitted with two differing loops, for suspension. The body is ornamented with a series of overlapping scales, arranged in four rows, with a band of archaic scrolls at the neck. Russet-brown and green patina. Han type; attributable to the Posterior Chou or Northern Sung Dynasty. Teakwood base.

275—SMALL ANCIENT BRONZE BELL

Bell: Height, 9 inches; width, 5½ inches.
With stand: Height, 15½ inches; width, 9½ inches.

Lenticular shape. The obverse and reverse present four oblong panels each, each of which holds four bosses, and a curved band of bosses passes below them on either face. Green and brownish patina in thick incrustations. Presumably a Shang or early Chou specimen. Has arched teakwood standard.

276—BRONZE HANGING VASE WITH COVER

Height, 8¼ inches; diameter, 7 inches.

Ovoid, with conventional tiger-head handles and rings, linked with chain and cross-bar for suspension. An ornamental band of archaic scrolling dragon forms encircling the middle is followed below by a twisted cord pattern. The remaining smooth surface is covered with a blended patina in rich tones of green and olive-brown. The homogeneous cover has two loose rings attached. Attributable to the Han Dynasty. The teakwood stand bears a gilt inscription; from Ch'ienlung's private collection to the present owner.

277—BRONZE SACRIFICIAL TRIPOD VESSEL

Height, 7½ inches; diameter, 6¼ inches.

Rounded body with upturned rim handles and three tubular feet. The main embellishment consists of a wide geometrical and latticed diaper band, in low relief, involving small flat dots to represent bosses. The upper border shows archaic dragon scrolls with similar fretting. Covered uniformly with a rich olive-brown and lustrous malachite (*shih lu*) patina. Interior has two Chou marks, impressed in the casting. Ascribable to the late Chou or early Han Dynasty. Has cover of teakwood, with carved jade ornament, and teakwood stand.

278—BRONZE SACRIFICIAL JAR

Height, 5½ inches; diameter, 10 inches.

Graceful rounded cup-shape, with projecting animal-head handles in conventional curves. Ornamented with an archaic scroll border below the rim, with conventional tiger masks on either side. A similar archaic border surrounds the base, with small vertical divisions at the sides. Rich olive-brown and verdigris-colored patina. On the interior of the bottom, an ancient incused mark. Chou type; attributable to the Han Dynasty. A similar example figures in the "Hsi Ch'ing Kü Chien" (catalogue of ancient bronzes), published in 1751 by order of the Emperor Ch'ien-lung. Has teakwood stand and cover, the latter mounted with a white jade ornament.

279—ANCIENT BRONZE SACRIFICIAL JAR

Height, 5 inches; diameter, 9½ inches.

Graceful rounded form with projecting monster-head handles holding ornamental loops with drops. Neck and base ornamented with small convoluted scrolls and fret, interrupted by vertical ridges below and conventional tiger masks above. The bulbous body is uniformly fluted, and a solid rich brown patina includes spottings of verdigris hue. Inscription on the interior. Fine Chou form; attributable to the Han Dynasty. Fitted teakwood stand and cover, the latter mounted with a carnelian agate ornament.

Note: A similar example figures in the "Hsi Ch'ing Kü Chien" catalogue of ancient bronzes, published in 1751, by order of Emperor Ch'ien-lung.

280—*ANGULAR BRONZE VESSEL WITH COVER*

Height, 6¾ inches; width, 10½ inches.

Oblong shape with slanting sides, raised on a beveled base with
arched openings. The incised ornament presents uniformly a delicately
interlaced pattern of serpentine scrolls, including that on the cover,
which is a reversed counterpart of the vessel itself. Dull greenish
patina. Attributable to the Han Dynasty. Has tall teakwood stand.

281—ANCIENT CYLINDRICAL BRONZE VASE

Height, 8 inches; diameter, 7¾ inches.

In the form of an upright spool with wide flanges. Archaic dragon-scroll and fret bands and monster-heads ornament the cylindrical body, and the flanges have incised gadroon borders. Fine patina of pale red, brown and green flecking. Fitted with a copper fire-pan or flower holder. Underneath the foot a mark meaning "left side," indicating probably that it was one of a set. Attributable to the T'ang or Sung era. Has teakwood stand.

282—ANTIQUE BRONZE TRIPOD VASE

Height, 10 inches; diameter, 7 inches.

Rounded caldron-shape, with three vertical dentated ridges, three tubular feet and two arched rim handles. The hieratic embellishment covering the entire body of the bronze between the ridges involves the admonitory ogre (*t'ao t'ieh yên*) lineaments, against a fretwork ground. The interior bears a Chou measure mark. Coated with a thickly incrusted patina in blended verdigris-green and brown tones. Han Dynasty. Has teakwood stand and cover, the latter surmounted by a jade bird ornament.

283—ANCIENT BRONZE SACRIFICIAL TRIPOD

Height, 7¼ inches: diameter, 8 inches.

With globular body, and arched handles on the outer rim. The full and rounded body, raised on three tapering feet, presents a massive, plain surface, with a richly blended patina, the incrustation including tones of malachite-green, russet-red and olive-brown. Attributable to the T'ang or Sung Dynasty. Has teakwood cover and stand.

284—ANCIENT BRONZE VASE

Height, 11½ inches; diameter, 6½ inches.

Quadrilateral, with ovated contour, contracted neck and short pyramidal base. Two of the sides present conventional mask handles with loops and loose rings; the remaining surfaces are plain and sustain a rich red and green patina. A typical example of the early Han era. Figured in ancient works on bronzes. Has teakwood stand.

285—ANCIENT BRONZE SACRIFICIAL JAR

Height, 6½ inches; diameter, 11½ inches.

Graceful rounded shape with projecting monster-head handles with curved loops and drops. The neck and low base sustain conventional archaic dragon-scroll borders, in low relief, and on the neck are grotesque masks. Patina showing olive-brown tones, with malachite-green zones. Similar examples figure only in the most noted collections. Attributable to the Han Dynasty. Has teakwood stand and cover, the latter mounted with a carved carnelian agate knob.

286—*ANTIQUE BRONZE TRIPOD*

Height, 10 inches; diameter, 7 inches.

Tripartite bulbous shape, with upturned angular handles at the rim, and raised upon three tall tapering feet. The archaic ornamentation in relief presents grotesque lineaments of animals, together with protuberant bosses on an impressed ground of recurrent fretwork. Shows a coating of brown patina and the remains of old gilding, and has a single-character mark meaning "high" or "great" treasure. Chou type; probably made during the Yüan or Ming eras. Has teakwood stand and cover, the latter with a carnelian agate ornament.

287—BRONZE SACRIFICIAL TRIPOD

Height, 7¼ inches; diameter, 9¼ inches.

Low, rounded body, on three feet with archaic masks, and with two angular upstanding rim handles. The surface embellishment presents a double bordering of archaic dragon-scrolls, impressed between lateral ridges. The exterior of this vessel shows a thickly incrusted patina of blended russet, brown and green tones. Attributable to the Han Dynasty. Has carved teakwood stand and cover.

288—ANCIENT BRONZE BEAKER

Height, 13⅛ inches; diameter, 7 inches.

Tall, with trumpet lip, slender body and narrow base. The middle section and the base bear vertical ridges and the admonitory *t'ao t'ieh yên* masks, on a ground of small impressed fretting. The remaining ornament beneath the neck consists of palmation forms. Red and green patina. Sung Dynasty. Has teakwood stand.

289—ANCIENT BRONZE TRIPOD WITH COVER

Height, 7¼ inches; diameter, 10 inches.

Globular (*Ting*) form with angular upturned handles, and raised on three plain curved legs. Originally used for sacrificial food in ancestor-worship ceremonies. Encircled by impressed bands of rope scroll and a projecting mid-band in elliptical bead forms. The bronze cover, with three rings, shows archaic dragon-scroll bordering. Richly mottled patina of russet-red and olive-brown tones. Fine example of the Chou Dynasty. Has teakwood stand.

290—ANCIENT BRONZE WINE VESSEL

Height, 11 inches; diameter, 11½ inches.

Flat pilgrim-bottle shape, with slightly raised elliptical panels on a low pyramidal base. On the shoulders small loops with loose rings. The smooth sides, without ornamentation, have a mottled patina showing soft tones of brown, red and green. Fine late Chou type; probably made during the early Han era. A similar example figures in one of the private native catalogues of ancient bronzes. Has teakwood stand.

291—LARGE GILT BRONZE DUCK CENSER

Height, 13½ inches; length, 11½ inches.

The duck is life size and is represented with open beak, walking on a rocky elevation surrounded by wave crests. Divided through the middle, the upper section forming the cover. Parcel gilt; where worn shows a coating of brown patina. Attributable to the Ming Dynasty.

292—COVERED BRONZE SACRIFICIAL TRIPOD VESSEL

Height, 10 inches with cover; width, 8⅝ inches.

Rounded, caldron-shaped body, raised on three curved feet with dragon-head knees, and with two arched rim handles. Impressed borders above and below a lateral ridge show fretted diaper and *lei-wên* (meander) motifs. The bronze cover, in low form, sustains a lion-crest center and three attached rings, and interlaced diaper and annular borders. Fine green patina. Attributable to the Sung Dynasty.

293—ANCIENT BRONZE TRIPOD WITH COVER

Height, 8½ inches; diameter, 10 inches.

Globular form, with two angular upturned handles near the rim, and raised on three plain curved feet. Originally used for sacrificial food in ancestor-worship. The exterior is embellished with intricate borders showing serpentine and dragon-head scrolls, and the original bronze cover carries similar scrolled borders, together with three ring handles. A rich patina of green and olive-brown. A similar form is illustrated in the "Hsi Ch'ing Ku Chien" (catalogue of ancient bronzes published in 1751 under the Emperor Ch'ien-lung). Fine Chou example. Has teakwood stand.

294—ANCIENT BRONZE SACRIFICIAL BOWL

Height, 6¼ inches; diameter, 9¾ inches.

Wide semi-globular shape with spreading base; used in remote periods for ceremonial offerings of grain or corn. The outer rim is bordered with archaic dragon-scrolls, interrupted by three conventional monster masks. A similar dragon scroll motif appears on the base, while the main surface presents a trellised design, with five rows of pointed *ju* (bosses), assumed to be ancient symbols of nutrition. The interior carries an inscription of two lines. The patina shows a fine blending of russet-red, brown and green tones. Attributable to the Chou Dynasty. Has carved teakwood stand and cover, the latter with carved jade ornament.

NOTE: A similar example figures in the famed collection of Baron Sumitome Paka.

295—*ANTIQUE DAMASCENED BRONZE VASE*

Height, 10⅜ inches; diameter, 8 inches.

Globular shape with flattened sides. The narrow rounded ends sustain at the shoulders grotesque animal heads, with loops and loose rings, a third loose ring appearing in front. The sides and ends are crossed by horizontal and vertical bands, damascened with gold and silver dragon-scrolls, which divide the surface of the body into four panels of impressed, wave-crested diapering in low relief. The attenuated neck has an inlaid leaf bordering, and the low oblong base sustains inlaid dragon borders to match the design of the cross bands. Fine Han shape; attributable to the T'ang or Sung Dynasty. Has teakwood stand.

296—*ANTIQUE BRONZE VESSEL*

Height, 8½ inches; diameter, 9 inches.

Wide oviform contour, with short neck, and two grotesque-head handles. The embellishment includes two bands with archaic scroll and boss motifs, and the broad shoulder carries an impressed ornamentation of convoluted scrolls, while the spaces below display a fretted net (*lo wên*) pattern, combined with bosses. The patina shows evenly blended tones of russet brown and green. Attributable to the Han Dynasty. Has teakwood stand.

297—GOLD-INCRUSTED BRONZE VASE

Height, 11¼ inches; diameter, 10½ inches.

Flattened pilgrim-bottle shape (*Ho*), with small round neck and
quadrangular base. The two narrow sides have mask handles and
loops, the flattened obverse and reverse presenting incrusted gold in
plain horizontal and intersecting vertical bands which form oblong divisions displaying dragon-scroll motifs. These are continued on the
narrow sides. Rich brown patina. Panel underneath bears date mark:
"Second month of the second year of Tê Ong's time." Han Dynasty.
Has teakwood stand.

298—INLAID BRONZE ANIMAL WINE VESSEL

Height, 10 inches; length, 13½ inches.

A mythological rhinoceros, called *hsi*, molded in hollow form to hold wine, such as were used for sacrificial purposes during the Chou Dynasty. The hinged lid on back shows a bird's head, which, like the collar around neck, the forehead, the eyes and tail, is studded with turquoise, whilst the body is enriched with gold and silver inlay in the form of large concentric scrolls. Rich patina of malachite-green. Attributed to the T'ang or early Sung Dynasty, but may be older. Has teakwood stand.

NOTE: A similar shape is illustrated in the "Hsi Ch'ing Ku Chien," published in 42 folio volumes, by direction of the Emperor Ch'ien-lung in 1751.

299—INLAID BRONZE WINE KETTLE

Height, 9 inches; diameter, 10 inches.

Low globular shape, with phœnix-head spout and dragon handle, linked to the neck, and with an open spiral work body. Raised on three small feet formed by bear-like figures, that support small phœnixes with outstretched wings. Body, encircled by bands of silver and gold inlaid dragon-scrolls, sustains contiguous fret patterns in linear bands delicately impressed in the original casting. The brown patina shows malachite-green zones. Interesting Chou shape; figured in several works on ancient Chinese bronzes. Probably made during the T'ang or Sung Dynasty. Has original bronze cover and modern teakwood stand.

300—INLAID BRONZE DUCK WINE VESSEL

Height, 13½ inches; length, 16½ inches.

Molded in conventional form; curving neck with beak serving for a graceful spout; handle linked to rim by small unicorns. The body has short rump feathers and rests on the web-feet. The *niellé* embellishment (known in China as *chin yin ssu*), shows archaic scrolls to suggest wings and feathers. The neck is encircled by a series of corded bands enclosing small raised rosettes. Patina of olive-brown and green tones. Han form; attributable to an early period of the Sungs. Has low teakwood stand.

301—INLAID BRONZE ANIMAL WINE VESSEL

Height, 10½ inches; length, 11 inches.

Molded in the hollow form of a mythical rhinoceros (*hsi*), with a vase on its back, to hold sacrificial wine (*ch'iu hsi tsun*). The inlaying over the quadruped's body and the surfaces of the wine beaker on its back is largely of archaic scrolls, executed in silver and gold niello, the rich patina including olive-brown and green tones. An early Chou type, figured in various works on old bronzes. Probably executed during the T'ang or Sung Dynasty. Has teakwood stand.

302—ANTIQUE BRONZE SACRIFICIAL JAR

Height, 7½ inches; diameter, 13 inches.

Graceful rounded form with lateral *arête* ridges and two projecting monster-head handles, on low spreading base; hieratic motifs in low relief, involving *t'ao t'ieh*, lineaments of the tiger, or gluttonous ogre, in conventional form. Base showing archaic dragon-scroll designs between the ridges. Dark olive-green patina. Ascribable to the close of the Han era. Impressed mark in interior of bottom. Fitted with teakwood cover and stand, the former having a jade elephant ornament.

303—ANCIENT BRONZE TRIPOD BOWL

Height, 9 inches; diameter, 11 inches.

Round, with angular upturned rim handles, and raised on three feet; ornamented with a bordering of detached *lei-wên* or "thunder scrolls." Richly mottled patina showing blended russet-red, brown and green tones. The interior has an ancient incuse mark in two characters—probably a name. Attributable to the Chou era. Has teakwood cover with jade ornament including a carved stand.

304—ANCIENT BRONZE VASE

Height, 12 inches; diameter, 8 inches.

Rare baluster-form with tapering neck and spreading base. The shoulder sustains two conventional monster-head handles with annular loops, while two smaller loops are attached to the neck above. Linear bands encircle the neck, shoulder and base. The patina shows deep brown and verdigris-green tones, with earthy incrustations from burial. Attributable to the Shang or early Chou Dynasty.

305—ANCIENT BRONZE VASE

Height, 13¾ inches; diameter, 7½ inches.

Quadrilateral, with contracted neck and swelling body. On two sides are conventional mask-like handles, with loops. The other sides are without ornament and all sustain a rich and mottled patina in olive-brown, russet-red and green tones. Ascribable to the Han Dynasty. Has teakwood stand.

306—UNIQUE STUDDED BRONZE VESSEL

Height, 7½ inches; diameter, 11½ inches.

Broad oviform, with contracted neck and slightly flaring rim. The rare ornamentation, aside from a serrated bordering of triangles on the shoulder, presents the oblique net pattern (*lo-wên*) in small impressed lozenge fretting and studded with turquoise bosses. Fine patina of russet-reds and greens. A Han type; attributed to a succeeding period. Has teakwood stand.

307—COVERED BRONZE SACRIFICIAL VESSEL WITH BASE

Height, 12¾ inches; diameter, 8¾ inches.

Shallow urn-shape, with openwork cover and separate base, the pierced designs uniformly showing flat undulating scrolls and small intersecting pierced details. The cover, of similar openwork, sustains three attached handles in recurved forms. The hexagonal bronze stand, with scrolled openwork panels, has a small railing. Coated uniformly with blended brown and green patina. Under side of cover bears an incised inscription with the name of the vessel, "Han P'an," and on the top of the middle section is another inscription. Attributed to the Han Dynasty. Fitted with extra teakwood stand.

308—ANTIQUE BRONZE TRIPOD VESSEL

Height, 12 inches; diameter, 10 inches.

Archaic coalescent shape with three tapering feet and two up-turned handles. The bulbous surface presents the lineaments of the admonitory (*haou-tëen*) ogre in low relief, while the neck is bordered by imbricated cloud scrolls in narrow bands. The incrusted old patina appears to be supplemented by touches of varied tones of lacquer. An interesting example, with an inscription of name (*Wang Ch'i mon?*) on the interior. Attributable to a period of the five dynasties succeeding the Han. Has carved teakwood stand and cover, the latter ornamented with an old carved jade knob.

309—ANCIENT BRONZE JAR WITH COVER

Height, 10½ inches; diameter, 13 inches.

Round, with projecting dragon-headed handles; on three feet with monster-head embellishments. The body presents a series of six grooved bands, followed above by an angular scroll border at the rim, and a bordering of gadroons finishes the base. The original cover, with similar grooves and ornament, is surmounted by a flanged knob. Rare patina of malachite, red and brown tints, and in parts thickly incrusted. Ascribable to the Chou Dynasty. Has teakwood stand with white jade plaquette center.

310—BRONZE SACRIFICIAL TRIPOD VESSEL

Height, 11 inches; diameter, 8½ inches.

Rounded body raised on three cylindrical legs, with two angular upstanding rim handles; the simple linear ornament consists of characteristic ancient meander bands in concentric scroll and key fretted forms. Exterior displays an unusually rich malachite (*shih-lu*) green patina with polished brilliancy. The interior is thickly covered with green incrustation, showing obscure incused mark—Chou type. Made toward the close of this dynasty—third or fourth century B.C. Has teakwood cover surmounted by an ancient jade ornament showing dragon and clouds delicately carved—fretted work. Stand of carved teakwood.

NOTE: A similar form is illustrated in the private catalogue of Baron Sumitome Paka

311

311—UNIQUE BRONZE SACRIFICIAL EWER WITH COVER

Height, 13¼ inches; length, 12 inches

Composite form of a mythological animal, propitiated as the queller of dragons and river monsters from the remote epoch of the Great Yü of Hsia, whose eulogy was handed down on a bronze ox. Cast in grotesque form, with bold relief details, including lizard-like dragons or *shih-lungs*, gluttonous-ogre lineaments, enormous tusks, huge mandibles, strongly defined eyes, outstanding ears and curling horns. The curved tail serves both for handle and as a fifth leg. The cover is formed by the upper part of the body, and bears lizard and mask-like presentments. The four legs, in tapering triangular form, suggest long tiger teeth. Coated with a rich olive-brown patina, showing slight variations of yellow and greenish tones.

This remrakable example appears to be unique, in technique and general conformation. Assumably of the Chou Dynasty. Has teakwood stand with white jade plaquette carved in relief with figures.

(Illustrated.)

312—ANTIQUE BRONZE WATER BOTTLE

Height, 14⅝ inches; diameter, 9 inches.

Graceful bottle-shape, with slender neck, bulbous six-lobed top and spreading body, without ornamentation, presenting a richly mottled patina of russet-red, brown and green hues. A similar bottle figures in the "Hsi Ch'ing Ku Chien" (catalogue of ancient bronzes, published under the Emperor Ch'ien-lung, in 1751), ascribed to the Chou Dynasty. This example may be attributed to the succeeding Han Dynasty.

313—LARGE BRONZE SACRIFICIAL JAR

Height, 10½ inches; diameter, 13 inches.

Broad oviform shape, with short neck and base and slightly flaring rim. On the shoulder are three symbolical ram's-head handles, while the remaining surface, with impressed ornament, presents angular and convoluted scrolls in the primitive form of the so-called *lei-wên* or "thunder scrolls," separated by three lateral ridges. Olive-green patina on the exterior, whilst in the interior the patina is blended with blue and verdigris green incrustations. Ascribable to the T'ang or Sung Dynasty.

314—SACRIFICIAL BRONZE HANGING JAR

Jar: Height, 12½ inches; diameter, 9 inches.
With stand: Height, 18¾ inches; width, 11 inches.

Semi-globular body, with broad neck and swinging handle for suspension (a form of vessel often presented by the old Emperors to deserving subjects); used for wine in the ceremonies of ancestor-worship. The ornamentation shows a simple geometrical diapered bordering at the shoulder, together with characteristic mask-like finials on the handle, and a loose cover. The original bronze cover bears a mark in Chou characters. Patina of russet-red, brown and malachite-green tones. Attributable to the Han Dynasty. Has teakwood stand, with an arch.

315—ANTIQUE BRONZE SACRIFICIAL JAR WITH COVER

Height, 13½ inches; diameter, 9½ inches.

Quadrangular shape with high, rounded shoulder, and of massive casting. On the shoulders are four ox-head handles. The whole is raised on the backs of four small ape-like figures, which serve as feet. Each of the four sides of the body is a network of small, sunken panels, filled with a geometrical oblique fret design, combined with small bosses. The short neck sustains a bordering of archaic dragon scrolls, and the original cover, with slanting sides, shows a geometrical (*lo-wên*) pattern to match the jar, and is surmounted by four grotesque bird forms. Deeply incrusted patina showing russet-red, green, brown and yellowish tones. Possibly a unique example of the Chou or Han era. Has teakwood stand.

316—ANCIENT BRONZE VASE WITH TIGERS

Height, 14 inches; diameter, 7½ inches.

Quadrilateral form with swelling sides; resting on four crouching tigers as feet, and sustaining tiger handles on two sides. Cast with vertical and horizontal cording interrupted by loose knots and enclosing panels enriched with sunken scroll work. The same sunken scroll motifs appear on the sides of the neck. Fine incrusted patina of olive-brown and green. Interesting and early Han example. Has teakwood stand.

317—*ANCIENT BRONZE VASE*

Height, 14½ inches; diameter, 8 inches.

Tall quadrangular shape with ovated contour and receding neck. and short, spreading base. Grotesque monster-head handles on two sides of the neck. The sunken ornament in linear border forms displays serpentine scrolls, succeeded below by a series of overlapping scale borders, arranged in three rows, while the base sustains archaic cloud scrolls. Mottled patina of green and olive-brown. Similar examples figure in native catalogues of ancient bronzes. Early Chou type. Attributable to the T'ang or Sung era. Has teakwood stand.

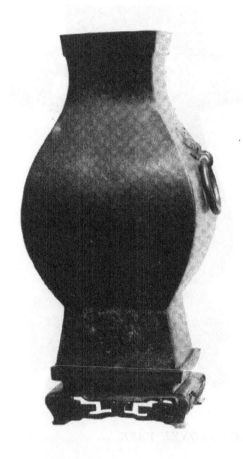

318—*ANCIENT BRONZE VASE*

Height, 14⅝ inches; diameter, 7⅞ inches.

Tall quadrangular shape with ovated contour and receding neck. Two sides presenting archaic ox-head handles with loops and suspended rings. The surfaces, without other ornament, present a richly mottled patina of russet-red, green and brown. A similar piece figures in one of the famed native catalogues of ancient bronzes. Attributed to the Han Dynasty. Has teakwood stand.

319—ANTIQUE BRONZE SACRIFICIAL BOWL

Height, 4½ inches; diameter, 15¾ inches.

Wide shallow form, with two angular rim handles; on circular spreading foot, the exterior presenting sunken ornamental bordering of celt-like forms. The interior bears an inscription of eight lines, in fine official script of the epoch. Rich patina of russet-red, brown and green tones. Late Chou or early Han. Has carved teakwood stand.

320—ANTIQUE INLAID BRONZE EWER WITH COVER

Height, 14½ inches; diameter, 8 inches.

Fashioned after an archaic sacrificial vessel, with three tapering feet, dragon-head handle and straight spout, the damascened embellishment in silver and gold presenting a triple lanceolation involving vague lineaments of the so-called *t'ao t'ieh* or gluttonous ogre. The original cover includes a bordering of like inlay in scroll ornament, and a narrow interlaced band near the knob. Brown and green patina. Ancient Chou form. Attributable to the T'ang or Sung era. Has teakwood stand.

321—UNIQUE NIELLO AND ENAMEL BRONZE VASE

Height, 14⅛ inches; diameter, 8⅛ inches.

Quadrangular shape with swelling body, receding neck and square base. The four sides, sustaining grotesque animal-mask handles with loops and loose rings, are enriched by gold and silver inlaying; green champlevé enamel, together with niello-work in geometrical design and inlaid gold dotting. The neck is encircled by a band of delicate fret design in silver wire. Patina showing deep olive-brown tones of even quality. Han type. Date uncertain; probably of the Sung era. Has teakwood stand.

322—LARGE ANTIQUE BRONZE VASE

Height, 14⅝ inches; diameter, 11 inches.

Bulbous body with receding neck and bell-shaped base, the base marked by vertical ridges, the shoulder sustaining two conventional monster-head handles with loops and free suspended rings. The embellishment, including a series of linear grooves and serrated leaf borderings, is completed at the neck by graven phœnix and fish emblems, together with an incuse inscription stating that this vessel was made by Mi Wong about two thousand years ago. The upper rim shows a pair of archaic dragons, rendered in sunken form. Blended patina with thick incrustations and malachite-green tones. Foot underneath bears raised mark in two ancient characters "Wong park." Attributed to the Han Dynasty. Has teakwood stand.

325

323—REMARKABLE BRONZE SACRIFICIAL JAR

Height, 8 inches; diameter, 18 inches.

Graceful circular form, sustaining projecting monster-head handles with curved loops and drops. The neck ornamented with a band in the form of "thunder scrolls," interrupted by two ox-head masks in relief, the larger surfaces of the rounded body presenting geometrical fretting centered with bosses. The base is finished by a "thunder scroll" motif similar to that of the neck. Interior inscribed with relief mark, meaning "long life." Patina of deep malachite-green tones. Rare Shang example, or possibly early Chou. Fitted with teakwood cover and stand, the former having a jade knob.

(Illustrated.)

324—LARGE BRONZE VASE WITH COVER

Height, 15½ inches; diameter, 9½ inches.

Bottle-shape with short, broad neck, and flanged base. Two conventional monster-head handles with loops and free rings at the shoulder, the remaining surface, with ornament, showing a rich patina with a blending of malachite and verdigris-green tones, thickly incrusted. In the interior of neck and base verdigris-green is intermingled with turquoise-blue. The bronze cover, with like patina, sustains four small symbolic animals like unicorns, to serve as handles. Figured in old native work on ancient bronze. Rare Han example. Has teakwood stand.

325—ANTIQUE DAMASCENED BRONZE VASE

Height, 14½ inches; diameter, 12 inches.

Quadrilateral with rounded edges, short receding neck and slightly spreading base. Two sides present grotesque projecting serpentine-headed handles. The damascened embellishment in gold and silver, presenting vigorous indulating scrolls and archaic dragon bands with bosses, is succeeded below by a series of four overlapping rows of scale patterns, extending uniformly about the four sides. On the base is a band of similar scales in gadroon form. Olive-brown patina of fine quality. Interior of neck bears an incised inscription giving the name of the vessel, "Goê Chüng Yuan Shang." Attributable to the T'ang or Sung era. Has teakwood cover with white jade ornament and rich teakwood stand.

(Illustrated.)

326—LARGE BRONZE SACRIFICIAL TRIPOD JAR

Height, 12 inches; diameter, 14 inches.

Round shape with arched handles attached to the outer rim. The body, raised on three curved feet, presents a series of border motifs, in impressed serpentine scrolls together with small spiral details. These bands are succeeded below by bordering of palmations. Fine patina of light olive tones. Ascribable to the Han Dynasty. Has teakwood stand and cover, the latter ornamented with a jade knob.

329

327—ANTIQUE BRONZE SACRIFICIAL JAR

Height, 10½ inches; diameter, 13 inches.

Wide globular form with short, broad neck, and three ram's-head handles on the shoulder, with an equal number of vertical ridges on the body below. Surface covered by archaic and convoluted scroll motifs, together with contiguous (*lei-wên*) fretted groundwork, relieved by three lateral ridges and concluding with a *lei-wên* meander band near base. Patina of olive-green tone. Attributable to the T'ang or Sung era.

328—ANTIQUE BRONZE VASE

Height, 13 inches; diameter, 9 inches.

Fine oviform with a short receding neck, and ring base; sustaining two conventional monster-head handles, with loops and loose rings at the shoulder, followed on the neck above by four smaller rings. On the body between successive grooves and ridges are five bands with a small intricate diaper pattern. The richly mottled patina shows incrusted verdigris-green and brownish tones. Attributable to the Han Dynasty. Has teakwood stand.

329—ANCIENT BRONZE BELL

Height, 14¾ inches; width, 11½ inches.
With stand: Height, 24½ inches; width, 16 inches.

Lenticular form with flat shoulder and a tubular top or handle. The two curved sides present a series of incuse fretted scroll bands, which alternate with pointed *ju*, or nipple-bosses, arranged in rows of three. The vertical central surface bears an incised inscription with the name of the founder. Coated with a blended brown and green patina. Similar bells are illustrated in native catalogues of ancient bronzes of the Chou Dynasty. Without clappers, such bells are struck from the outside, with hardwood mallets. Has arched teakwood standard for suspension.

(Illustrated.)

330—LARGE BRONZE TRIPOD JAR WITH COVER

Height, 11½ inches; diameter, 14 inches.

Low globular shape, with two arched handles on outer rim; raised on three curving feet. (Used originally for sacrificial ceremonies and ancestor-worship.) The exterior surface is ornamented with two broad borders, which uniformly display archaic dragon motifs in scrolling forms, in low relief, together with small spiral details. The cover, with three annular attachments, sustains similar borderings of dragon-scrolls in low relief. Invested with a fine patina of olive-green tones, showing russet-red flecking. Chou type; ascribable to the Han era. Has teak-wood stand.

332

333

331—ANTIQUE BRONZE CLOCK

Height, 15¾ inches; diameter, 8½ inches.

Quadrangular, with ovated contour, straight flanged base, and short receding neck; the four sides holding conventional mask handles with loops and loose rings. The sides uniformly display large archaic scrolls, midst a field of small dragon-diapering. Thickly incrusted brown patina. Characteristic Han example. Has teakwood stand.

332—ANCIENT BRONZE VASE

Height, 14 inches; diameter, 14 inches.

Broad ovoid body with attenuated neck, spreading lip, and slightly spreading base. Ornamented with cording, tied so as to form a double series of panelings, enclosing small wave and diaper fret patterns, in miniature. Blended patina of olive-brown and green tones. A fine Han example. Has teakwood stand.

(Illustrated.)

333—ANCIENT BRONZE TRIPOD JAR WITH COVER

Height, 12½ inches; diameter, 12 inches.

Broad globular (*Ting*) form with two angular rim handles, and curving feet. Used originally for sacrificial food in ancestor-worship. Exterior embellishment presenting a series of impressed linear borders, with small vermiform scrolls suggesting archaic dragon motifs, with a leaf band below the borders separated by a horizontal median ridge. The bronze cover, with similar fretted and scroll bordering, is surmounted by a flanged knob. Invested with a thick incrusted and soft green-toned patina. Chou type; attributable to the close of that era, or to the following Han Dynasty. Has teakwood stand.

(Illustrated.)

334—ANCIENT BRONZE TIGER GONG

Height, 16½ inches; diameter, 9 inches.

Tall inverted jar shape, tapering downward from the bulbous shoulder. The flat lid-formed top sustains a walking tiger to serve as a handle for suspension. The base underneath is left open for the emission of sound. Fashioned without ornament, the body presents a mottled olive-brown patina, with blended incrustations of rare malachite tints. Similar examples figure in native works on ancient bronzes attributed to the Chou Dynasty. Has teakwood stand.

335—LARGE DAMASCENED BRONZE VASE

Height, 16 inches; diameter, 13½ inches.

Tall oviform with flaring neck, the shoulder sustaining two loop
handles with conventional animal-heads, followed below by a third
handle on one face. The damascened embellishment in silver and gold,
presenting a series of archaic borders in recurrent scroll design, is succeeded below by a serrated leaf bordering which vaguely displays the
ogre lineaments. The blended patina includes russet-red, brown and
green tones. Interior of neck sustains as an inscription the seal of a
high official, with the name Wong Tou. Ascribed to the T'ang or Sung
Dynasty. Has carved teakwood stand.

337

338

336—LARGE COPPER-INCRUSTED BRONZE VASE

Height, 18½ inches; diameter, 13 inches.

Molded in ovated shape with low spreading base and two bird-head side handles projecting from the neck. Body with inlaid copper embellishment presenting a series of four panels on either face, uniformly ornamented with archaic dragon scrolls, together with linear bordering; the neck is surrounded by key-fret and serrated bands, the base finished in dragon panels. Has a rich olive-brown patina of even tonality. Attributable to the Han Dynasty. Has carved teakwood stand.

337—ANTIQUE BRONZE VASE

Height, 16½ inches; diameter, 12½ inches.

Oviform with attenuated neck, sustaining two conventional monster-head handles with annular loops at the shoulder. The bulbous body presents wide braided or cord meshes at the horizontal and vertical intersections of bands of cording which form panels that separately disclose small impressed dragon scrolls. Blended patina of russet and brown tones. Attributable to the Five Short Dynasties, or pro-T'ang era. Has teakwood stand.

(Illustrated.)

338—LARGE BRONZE TRIPOD BOWL

Height, 17 inches; diameter, 16½ inches.

Deep rounded form, with angular upturned handles at rim. Raised on three curved feet, which are ornamented with ogre lineaments and dentated ridges. The body has raised border designs involving interlaced dragon-scroll motifs. These patterns are divided by six vertical protruding ridges and a horizontal twisted or corded band; another bordering in leaf form follows below. Rich mottled patina of light olive-green. Interior sustains an incuse inscription in tablet form and hieroglyphics, the cryptic and admonitory meanging of which is not readily decipherable. Ascribable to the Han era. Fitted with massive teakwood stand.

(Illustrated.)

339—LARGE ANTIQUE BRONZE VASE

Height, 17⅜ inches; diameter, 14 inches.

Broad, globular body with tapering neck, supporting two conventional monster-head handles with loose rings. The remaining surface, without other embellishment, presents a rich mottled patina, including blended russet, olive-brown and malachite- or verdigris-green tones. Fine Han example. Illustrated in native books on ancient bronzes. Has massive carved teakwood stand.

(Illustrated.)

340—INLAID BRONZE ANIMAL-FORM VESSEL ON WHEELS

Height, 14¾ inches; length, 19½ inches.

Representing a mythological ram, on four wheels; used on altars during the performance of the ancestor-worship ceremonies. The small cover on the back has a cicada fly, as a knob, and the horns on the head are in the round. The body shows oxidized silver incrustations in scrolled bands to suggest the wool, while bold spiral gold inlay outlines the leg joints. Brown patina. Large and rare; attributable to the T'ang or Sung Dynasty. Similar examples figure in native books on bronzes. Has carved stand.

(Illustrated.)

341—ANCIENT BRONZE BELL

Height, 19 inches; width, 12 inches.
With stand: Height, 31 inches; width, 19 inches.

Lenticular shape with narrow cylindric top for suspension; edges slightly curved. The convex obverse and reverse present varied incuse inscriptions of dedication to the sun and moon, with special names of Long Chung and Ho Shang, together with rows of *ju* or pointed nipple bosses, arranged in the usual order of three rows, and eighteen to the side. The upper section shows cloud scrolls. Blended olive-brown and green patina. This bell is probably unique, though similar in form to those figured in ancient bronze catalogues. Attributable to the Chou Dynasty. Has an arched teakwood stand for suspension.

(Illustrated.)

339

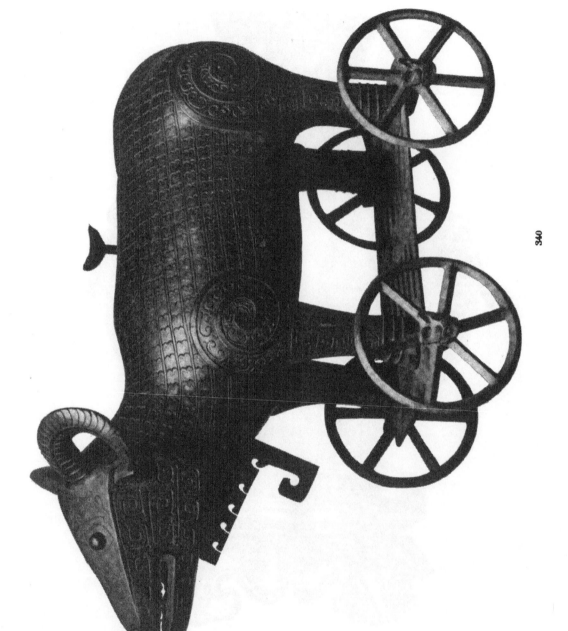

340

342—TALL BRONZE TRIPOD COLANDER, OR YEN

Height, 19¾ inches; diameter, 12 inches.

Ancient composite (*hsien*) shape, used for steaming grain or herbs at sacrificial ceremonies; with arched rim handles; surmounting a bulbous tripod with tapering feet, which display in bold relief the *t'ao t'ieh yên*, or ogre lineaments. The upper section of the vessel is encircled by an archaic dragon-scroll band in low relief. The interior bears an old incuse inscription. Deep incrusted patina displaying blended russet-red, brown and malachite hues of unusual quality. This remarkable Shang type may be attributed to the Chou or early Han era. Has massive carved teakwood stand and cover, the latter mounted with an old white jade ornament.

(Illustrated.)

343—REMARKABLE BRONZE VASE

Height, 19½ inches; diameter, 12 by 10 inches.

Tall quadrangular shape with flattened neck and swelling body, with two free projecting monster-head handles. The archaic ornament in relief presents the lineaments of the *haou tëen* or admonitory tiger head, well defined by vigorous lines against a small-fretted ground. Neck and base display bold serpentine scrolls, suggestive of the primitive evolution of the tiger and dragon conflict. Incrusted patina, showing malachite and other green tones, midst earthy agglomerations from long burial. Similar examples are illustrated in native books on old bronzes, but this example appears to be unique. Attributable to the close of the Chou period. Has carved teakwood stand.

(Illustrated.)

344—LARGE ANCIENT BRONZE GONG

Height, 30½ inches; width, 19 by 16 inches.
With stand: Height, 43 inches; width, 27½ inches.

Tall ovated jar-shape tapering downward from the bulbous shoulder. The flat lid-top, which is fastened to the rim, supports a tiger, to serve as a handle for suspension, the base underneath being left open for the emission of sound. Fashioned without ornament, the surface presenting a deep brown patina with thick incrustations. A similar example of the Chou Dynasty figures in the "Hsi Ch'ing Ku Chien," published under Emperor Ch'ien-lung. Has arched teakwood standard for suspension.

(Illustrated.)

345—JEWELED TIBETAN GILT BRONZE STATUETTE

Height, 6½ inches; width, 3¼ by 3¼ inches.

Representing Kuan-yin (Avalōkitês-vara), the Chinese goddess of mercy, seated upon a lotus thalamus. The deity in traditional pose is shown with elongated ears of Buddhahood, clad in rich attire, and wearing a tiara with a jeweled setting. Mounted on gilt bronze base studded with jewels. Date: Early XVIth century. Ta Ming Dynasty. Extra teakwood stand with silver wire inlaying.

346—GILT BRONZE STATUETTE

Height, 8½ inches; width, 5 by 6 inches.

Representing a seated Buddhist priest, whose flowing robes are enriched with chased bordering; shaven head, long ear lobes, and hands in traditional pose. This image has a gilt bronze base with a flaming "sun-ger" (*fanagoko*) or "black plaque," in arched form. The figure shows earthy incrustations from burial. Bears a mark; attributable to the Ming Dynasty.

347—JEWELED GILT BRONZE BIRD VASE

Height, 7½ inches; width, 6 by 5½ inches.

Presenting a pair of megapodes or "jungle fowl," resting upon a rustic base, surrounded by herbage; with hollowed mount between them, forming the vessel. Parcel gilt plumage is carefully indicated by chasing, while wings and receptacle are incrusted with varied semi-precious hard-stones. Era of Ch'ien-lung (1736-1795).

348—PAIR OF CLOISONNÉ CANDLESTICKS

Height, 13¾ inches; diameter, 5 inches.

Conventional tubular form, with prickets. The cloisonné enamel with turquoise-blue ground, showing arabesque scrolls, and lotus flowers. Circular "shou" marks and archaic dragon motifs appearing on bell-shaped bases; including parcel gilding mounting. Date: Ta Ch'ing Dynasty.

341

342

349—*MING CLOISONNÉ ENAMEL VASE*

Height, 14⅝ inches; diameter, 11 inches.

Broad globular form with tapering neck and spreading base; shoulder sustaining grotesque animal-head handles and enameled rings. The cloisonné enamel embellishment presents a deep turquoise ground with a pair of lapis-blue dragons in pursuit of the sacred pearl, midst conventional red nebulæ, scrolls, and varicolored cloud patches. The neck sustains a like turquoise-blue ground, with a purple grapevine motif enclosed between an imbricated leaf border and a blue band with plum blossoms in varied colors. The base shows a wave pattern and horses. Ming Dynasty; probably Wan-li. Has teakwood stand.

350—*LARGE CLOISONNE ENAMEL VASE*

Height, 18 inches; diameter, 8½ inches.

Bottle-shape, with tall slender neck sustaining two enameled handles in fabulous phœnix-bird design. The cloisonné embellishment with turquoise-blue ground presenting floral designs in varied colors together with lapis-blue lanceolated bordering. Around the body are four circular medallions with *shou* characters in turquoise and lapis-blue tones, enclosed by a ring of jet black. Date: Early Ch'ien-lung (1736-1795). Has teakwood stand.

351—*LARGE MING CLOISONNÉ ENAMEL VASE*

Height, 21½ inches; diameter, 14 inches.

Bulbous pear-shape with grotesque bird-head handles and loose bronze rings. The cloisonné embellishment, with rich turquoise-blue ground, presents a pair of dragons rising from the sea in quest of the sacred jewel, midst nebulæ and small cloud patches, uniformly rendered in several colors. The receding neck displays conventional lotus flowers in typical colors, separated by narrow blue and flowered bands from the upper grapevine motifs. Date: Wan Li period. Ta Ming Dynasty.

352—*LARGE CLOISONNÉ TEMPLE SET*

Consisting of five pieces, viz.:

A: LARGE INCENSE BURNER, forming the center-piece, fashioned in quadrangular shape, with four tubular feet that sustain cloisonné enamel embellishment and gilt bronze dragon-heads; two arched handles finish the upper rim. The body, including corner and side ridges, presents cloisonné motifs in archaic design and varied light colors on a turquoise-blue ground. Oblong cover, with similar cloisonné embellishment, surmounted by a large gilt bronze knob with openwork in dragon and cloud design. Ta Ch'ing Dynasty.

Height, 19 inches; width, 12 inches.

B: PAIR OF PRICKET CANDLESTICKS, in rectangular form, with spreading base, and cloisonné embellishment on a turquoise-blue ground.

Height, 16½ inches.

C: PAIR OF BEAKERS, quadrangular shape, with spreading neck and base sustaining cloisonné leaf bordering on a turquoise-blue ground, to match the preceding objects. Teakwood stand for each.

Height, 16 inches.

343

344

353—CLOISONNÉ ENAMEL AND GILT BRONZE ALTAR SET

Garniture of five pieces, comprising:

A: OBLONG INCENSE BURNER, with two gilt dragon handles, and four gilt (dragon-headed) feet to match. The sides presenting cloisonné floral and fret designs in varied brilliant colors, on turquoise-blue ground. Shoulder finished with gilt bronze gadroon bordering. Dome-shape cover of gilt bronze openwork, enriched with champlevé enamel in colors, is surmounted by a large gilt bronze coiling dragon knob with openwork cloud forms. Era of Ch'ien-lung (1736-1795).

Height, 12¾ inches; width, 9 inches with handles; body, 6 inches by 5 inches.

B: PAIR OF BEAKERS, to match. Quadrangular shape. The cloisonné decoration showing turquoise-blue ground with palmation, lotus flowers and mask designs.

Height, 9½ inches; width, 4⅞ by 4⅞ inches.

C: PAIR OF PRICKET CANDLESTICKS, with similar turquoise-blue ground and floral motifs in varied colors, including gilt gadroon borders, to match the preceding objects.

Height, 10½ inches.

All fitted with teakwood stands.

(Illustrated.)

354—TALL MING CLOISONNÉ VASE WITH CLOCK

Height, 21½ inches; width, 11½ by 9 inches.

Flattened quadrangular shape with ovated contour and grotesque phœnix-bird handles, enriched by turquoise-blue enameling. Obverse side (holding white enameled dial in Roman notation) presents archaic lapis-blue dragons and phœnix-head scrolls on turquoise-blue ground, supplemented with rosette forms. The reverse displays a cloisonné panel with figure of a mandarin and two attendants, who carry disks bearing the character meaning "happiness." Neck is encircled by escalloped bordering together with fretted corner palmations—while a meander and serrated border, in varied colors, on turquoise-blue ground finishes the base. Ta Ming Dynasty.

Rounded semi-globular form with arched rim handles; raised on three tubular feet, the cloisonné design, on turquoise-blue ground, presenting a double bordering of angular dragon scrolls, followed below by a bordering of descending escalloped forms, with archaic design, involving mask-like details; followed below by green flowered diaper pattern. The three legs present dragon scrolls similar to the body. Early Ch'ien-lung. Teakwood stand with cover.

356—LARGE CLOISONNÉ INCENSE BURNER

Height, 27 inches (with cover); width, 16 by 14 inches.

Quadrangular shape with vertical dentated ridges at sides and corners; two arched and enameled rim handles; oblong body raised on four archaic gilt bronze legs, designed to represent leaping fish. The cloisonné embellishment presents gluttonous ogre lineaments, copied from ancient bronzes, rendered in rich enamels on a ground of deep turquoise-blue, with varied borders. The domed cover, of gilt bronze with cloisonné, involves openwork bat and cloud motifs, and is surmounted by a grotesque lion. Has teakwood stand.

357—TWO LARGE CLOISONNÉ PALACE INCENSE BURNERS

Height, 36 inches; width, 20 by 16 inches. Total height, 42 inches.

Quadrilateral shape with vertical *arête* ridges at corners and sides, and two arched rim handles. Raised on four grotesque gilt bronze fish-dragon feet, with cloisonné embellishment; the body presenting archaic *haou tëen* or ogre-mask motifs in cloisonné designs copied from ancient bronzes, in varied colors on a turquoise-blue ground. The upper band shows lapis-blue and yellow dragon scrolls. The dome-shape covers of gilt bronze sustain dragon motifs and green enameled disk symbols, and have grotesque lion finials. Oblong teakwood stands.

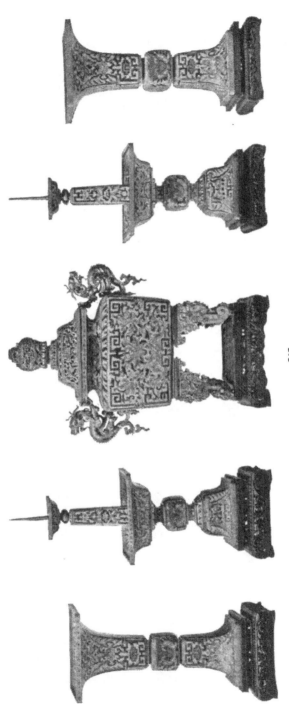

353

368

358—CHAMPLEVÉ AND GILT BRONZE ALTAR SET

Garniture de cheminée of five pieces, comprising:

A: LARGE INCENSE BURNER, quadrifoliate shape with dragon handles; raised on four monster-head feet. Parcel-gilt copper, enriched with champlevé enameling to represent quartz, turquoise and lapis-lazuli, together with coral incrustations, in floral and escalloped designs including bats and circular *shou* devices, meaning happiness and longevity. Has teakwood cover with carnelian agate ornament. Date: Era of Ch'ien-lung (1736-1795).

Height, 18½ inches; width, 13 inches.

B: PAIR OF BEAKERS, hexagonal shape, of repoussé gilt copper and incrusted enamel lotus flowers, with borderings to match.

Height, 13 inches; diameter, 7 inches.

C: PAIR OF PRICKET CANDLESTICKS, of gilt copper with similar turquoise, lapis and coral floral designs and borders.

Total height, 16¾ inches.

Teakwood stands for the set.

(*Illustrated.*)

359—TWO LARGE JEWELED AND GILT BRONZE CAKE BOXES

Height, 5½ inches; diameter, 12½ inches.

Low circular shape; cover and sides displaying delicately chased bordering in intricate swastika and "T" fret patterns, enriched by ruby and brilliant glass studding. Center of cover sustaining a stellated rosette design, jeweled in emerald and amethyst-colored glass, surrounded by four emblematical bats in ruby-like setting. Date: Ta Ch'ing Dynasty. Have teakwood stands.

(*Illustrated.*)

360—TWO LARGE JEWELED GILT BRONZE WALL VASES

Height, 16 inches; width, 8¾ inches.

Gourd-shape with flat back. Ornate designs in gilt bronze, including ruby and sapphire-colored glass, in wreath and border motifs. Each section enclosing a medallion with a gilt character (*Ta keih*) meaning "great prosperity." The gourds symbolize long life. Ta Ch'ing Dynasty.

(*Illustrated.*)

361—TWO GILT BRONZE AND CHAMPLEVÉ LANTERNS

Height, 23 inches; width, 10 by 8 inches.

Tall double-lozenge form, with painted glass faces and open sides. Raised from their bases on slender stems and surmounted by pagoda-like domes of openwork gilt bronze. Champlevé enamel embellishment, showing delicate bordering and wave motifs. Obverse and reverse hold swastika emblems. The domed tops are crowned by lapis-lazuli spheres, and the glass panels are lined with green silk. Era of Ch'ien-lung (1736-1795). Has teakwood stand.

362—PAIR OF TALL CLOISONNÉ TEMPLE LANTERNS

Height, 25½ inches; width, 8 by 8 inches.

Quadrilateral shapes, with ornate reticulated gilt bronze details and cloisonné-colored enameling on turquoise-blue ground. Central section showing truncated corners in fretted designs with slanting ends; sustaining glass panels on four sides; uniformly painted with sacred white elephant subjects. Upper section, or covering, fashioned to resemble a tilted roof, with pierced work of gilt bronze and cloisonné enameling; topped by a small gilt bronze dome. The base shows small gilt bronze balustrades and openwork, together with cloisonné enameled arabesque motifs on turquoise-blue ground. Era of Ch'ien-lung (1736-1795).

363—LARGE GILT BRONZE CLOCK

Height, 30 inches; width, 18 by 14 inches.

Round white enamel dial with Roman numerals; raised on four ornamental scroll feet and mounted upon a square, massive base, the latter, with European and Chinese designs, sustaining gilt bronze railing and dragon brackets at the four corners. Mechanical performing acrobats and jugglers. Hand-made movement with chimes.

364—LARGE GILT BRONZE CLOCK

To match the preceding.

NOTE: The above clocks were presented to Prince Kung (Kung Ching Wang) by Bow Chung Tang, a former Prime Minister, during the reign of Hsien Feng or T'ing-chih (1851-1874).

360

359

360

ENTRANCE TO IMPERIAL PRINCE KUNG'S PALACE GROUNDS

THIRD AND LAST AFTERNOON'S SALE

SATURDAY, MARCH 1, 1913

AT THE AMERICAN ART GALLERIES

BEGINNING AT 2.30 O'CLOCK

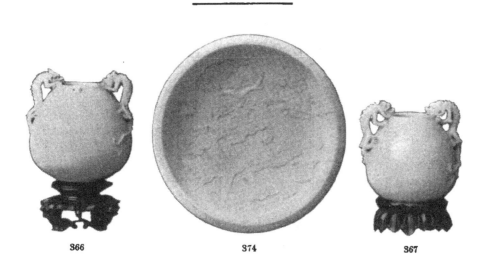

366   374   367

365—SMALL SOFT-PASTE WATER COUPE

Shallow rounded form, the delicate relief modeling presenting floral motifs and butterflies, the decoration being completed at the neck by a stellated bordering. Soft white glazing. Era of Yung Ch'êng (1723-1735). Teakwood stand.

366—WHITE SOFT-PASTE PORCELAIN COUPE

Ovate shape, with two *shih-lung* dragons forming handles, their heads surmounting the rim and cleft tails spreading on the sides. Delicately modeled, and coated with soft white glazing. Era of Yung Ch'êng (1723-1735).

367—WHITE PORCELAIN COUPE IN HARD PASTE

Ovate shape, with two *shih-lung* dragons forming handles, their heads surmounting the rim and cleft tails spreading on the sides. Pellucid white glazing. Era of Yung Ch'êng (1723-1735).

368—WHITE SOFT-PASTE WATER COUPE

Graceful rounded form; embellishment displaying small butterflies in delicate relief under ivory-white glazing with small crackle. Era of Yung Ch'êng (1723-1735). Has teakwood stand.

369—SOFT-PASTE SEAL COLOR-BOX

Round shape, termed *yin sê ho*. With a decoration of dragons mid swirling waves, in low relief, the cover having an ivory-toned glaze, and the glaze of the lower section including light drab clouding. Hsüan-Tê type. Ascribable to the era of Yung Ch'êng (1723-1735). Teakwood stand.

370—SMALL WHITE SOFT-PASTE WATER COUPE

Rounded form with wide aperture, the low-relief ornamentation presenting a squirrel and grape-vine motif, under the ivory-white glaze, with delicate crackle. Era of Yung Ch'êng (1723-1735). Has teakwood stand.

371—WHITE TING YAO WATER COUPE

Shallow conical form; delicately raised embellishment showing lotus flowers with foliations under a soft ivory-white glazing with small crackle. Late Sung or Yuan Dynasty. With stand.

372—WHITE SOFT-PASTE BOX WITH COVER

Shallow rounded form, the cover slightly flattened and displaying a dragon rampant, midst delicate cloud scrolls, enclosed by a narrow convoluted cloud-scroll bordering, which is repeated on the lower surface of the bowl. Glaze showing grayish tones and a small crackle. Era of Yung Ch'êng (1723-1735). Teakwood stand.

373—THIN WHITE SOFT-PASTE PORCELAIN COUPE

Diameter, 3½ inches.

Shallow rounded form with contracted upper rim. Delicate porcelain of egg-shell lightness, sustaining convoluted cloud-scrolls and a hairline border next to the rim, finely incised under the glaze. Early Ch'ien-lung. Teakwood stand.

374—WHITE SOFT-PASTE PORCELAIN COUPE

Diameter, 4⅜ inches.

Shallow rounded form, the exterior displaying the so-called "orange-peel" surface, and a bordering at the rim in convoluted fungiform. Interior decorated with a rampant dragon and cloud motifs, in low relief. Ivory-white glaze, with small crackle. Era of Yung Ch'êng (1723-1735). Teakwood stand.

375—WHITE SOFT-PASTE BOX WITH COVER

Diameter, 4¼ inches.

Shallow, circular form, the cover sustaining an Imperial five-clawed dragon rising from the sea, a similar wave decoration finishing the outer surface of the bowl. Era of Yung Ch'êng (1723-1735). Teakwood stand.

376—PURE WHITE PORCELAIN VASE

Height, 5½ inches.

Graceful ovated form with small neck. Fine Ta Ch'ing porcelain, ornamented with "*fu* lion" and symbolical *chu* or ball, with fillets, rendered in delicate relief under the glaze. Era of Yung Ch'êng (1723-1735).

377—IVORY-WHITE VASE

Height, 6 inches.

Ovoid, with small neck; fine cabinet example, showing a soft ivory-white glaze, with delicate crackle. Attributable to the later Sung or Yuan Dynasty. Teakwood stand.

378—IVORY-WHITE BOTTLE

Height, 7¾ inches.

Double-gourd shape, with elongated neck; cabinet example showing ivory-toned glazing with delicate crackle. Attributable to the Yuan Dynasty. Has teakwood stand.

379—PAIR OF OLD IVORY-WHITE FU LIONS

Height, 10½ inches; width, 5½ by 4½ inches.

These Buddhistic creatures, raised on open quadrangular bases, are strongly modeled in buff-colored clay, showing open muzzles and collars with bells; they have curly, strap-like manes. Mottled ivory-white glaze. Rendered in usual form with right paw resting on the symbolical ball *chu*. Sung Dynasty.

380—IVORY-WHITE PILGRIM BOTTLE

Height, 7 inches.

Flattened, with short cylindrical neck sustaining relief handles. Delicately raised bat and flower motifs, enclosed by "thunder scroll" bordering on obverse and reverse. Ivory-white glaze, showing a slight clouding, with a minute crackle texture. Attributable to the Sung Dynasty. Teakwood stand.

381—WHITE ORNAMENTED CABINET VASE

Height, 7¼ inches.

Bulbous oviform with receding neck, which sustains an escalloped overhanging collar. Fine Ta Ch'ing porcelain with low relief ornamentation presenting varied symbolical flowers and foliations, enclosed above and below by lanceolated and gadroon borderings; neck surrounded by ascending leaf border. Era of Ch'ien-lung. Teakwood stand.

382—BLANC-DE-CHINE COUPE

Diameter, 6 inches.

Vitreous white paste fashioned to resemble a priest's alms bowl, and presenting a light ivory-toned glazing without ornament. Attributable to the early XVIIth century. Including delicately carved stand.

383—WHITE TING YAO TRIPOD CENSER

Height, 6 inches.

Globular form with flanged neck and raised upon three lion-headed feet; fashioned after an ancient bronze sacrificial vessel. Ivory-white glaze. Carved teakwood cover, with agate knob. Late Sung or Yuan Dynasty.

384—WHITE YUNG LO BOWL

Diameter, 7¾ inches.

Wide form with small indentations at rim. Translucent thin
bossing (*t'o-t'ai*), the interior showing delicately raised serpentine
band and Buddhistic emblems of good augury, slightly raised under
the pellucid glazing, and the *k'uan* seal mark in four ancient characters imbedded in the paste. Made era Yung Lo (1403-1425),
Ming Dynasty. Teakwood stand.

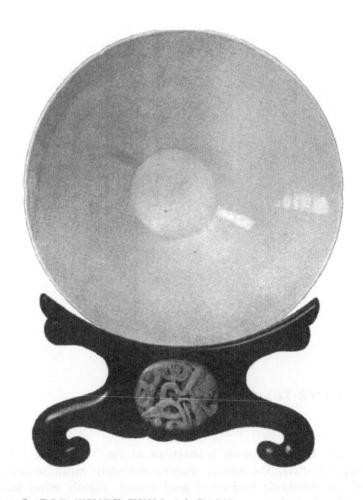

385—LARGE WHITE YUNG LO BOWL

Diameter, 8⅝ inches.

With flaring form, with the usual small indentations at the rim;
translucent egg-shell porcelain (*t'o-t'ai yao*). Interior showing the
eight Buddhistic emblems in delicate relief modeling under the glaze,
the interior of bottom a four-character mark: "Yung Lo nien-chih"
(1403-1424), of the Ming Dynasty. Teakwood stand with carved
white jade medallion.

386—TWO IVORY-WHITE BOTTLES

Height, 9 inches; diameter, 5½ inches.

Inflated pilgrim-bottle form without handles. *Fên Ting yao;* embellished with impressed rampant dragons, midst cloud forms that suggest sacred *ling-chih*, the old ivory white glazing showing mauve zones. Sung or Yuan Dynasty. Teakwood stand.

387—LARGE WHITE SUNG BOWL

Diameter, 9¼ inches.

Ancient form, with narrow metal rim, the interior presenting lotus flowers and scrolling foliations in delicate relief under a "rice-white" glazing. Exterior without ornamentation, glazed in like tone. **Sung Dynasty.** Teakwood stand.

388—*TWO LARGE WHITE FRUIT DISHES*

Diameter, 11¾ inches.

Shallow circular shape, finished with a narrow metal rim. Interior decoration presenting a lotus flower motif in delicate relief, which surrounds the central medallion together with a narrow band of fretting. Exterior without ornament. Uniform rice-colored glazing. Sung Dynasty.

389—PURE WHITE PORCELAIN BOTTLE

Height, 8⅝ inches.

Unique form with high rounded shoulders simply embellished with two projecting goat-like heads that suggest handles. Fine Ta Ch'ing porcelain of clear hard texture, uniformly covered with a milk-white glaze. Early Ch'ien-lung (1736-1795). Has teakwood stand.

390—WHITE SOFT-PASTE VASE

Height, 12¼ inches.

Pear shape with wide neck; ornamented with a conventional fruit and floral motif in low relief under a soft ivory-toned crackled glaze. The decoration is completed at the neck by lanceolated fungus heads, narrow fretting and upstanding leaves. Era of Ch'ien-lung (1736-1795).

391—WHITE TING YAO BOWL

Diameter, 8⅛ inches.

Ancient form finished with narrow copper rim. The interior decoration, in delicate relief, presents a wide bordering enclosing lotus flowers and ducks, carefully outlined on a ground of small concentric scrolls. The central panel contains a pair of symbolical fishes posed upon a ground of sea-wave pattern. The exterior is without ornament. The glazing shows a mellowed ivory tone. Sung Dynasty. Has high teakwood stand.

392—BLANC-DE-CHINE STATUE

Height, 13¼ inches.

Standing figure of Kwan-yin, the compassionate hearer of prayers; beautifully modeled in vitreous Fuchien ware which sustains a creamy white glazing of uniform quality. The divinity, clad in flowing drapery, and showing a serene countenance, with the usual long ear lobes of a Bodhisattva, is adorned with a necklace, tiara and hood. Delicately molded fingers. Ming Dynasty.

393—BLANC-DE-CHINE STATUETTE

Height, 12¼ inches.

Representing Kwan-yin, the compassionate hearer of prayers.
Vitreous *Fuchien yao*. The divinity is seated upon an open rockery,
clad in loose, flowing drapery, with serene features, and long ear-lobes,
and the *urna* mark of a Bodhisattva on her forehead. The hands, with
delicate, long finger nails, hold the sacred scroll. Uniformly glazed in
cream-white of velvety quality. Ming dynasty.

394—BLANC-DE-CHINE STATUETTE

Height, 12¼ inches.

Kwan-yin (the Maternal), seated upon rocky elevation, holding a Buddha-child on her knee—symbol of innocence. The deity is modeled in flowing loose robes of an ancient period. Fuchien ware of vitreous quality with a light cream-colored glaze. Ming Dynasty.

395—TALL BLANC-DE-CHINE STATUE

Height, 17¼ inches.

Kwan-yin, beautifully modeled in standing position. Vitreous white *Fuchien yao*, coated with a cream-white glaze of soft velvety quality. The divinity, in flowing drapery, is standing upon a rocky eminence, and wears a necklace and pendant and the usual head covering. Ming Dynasty.

396—RARE OSTRICH-EGG PORCELAIN VASE

Height, 13 inches.

Fine ovoid shape, without embellishment, presenting a shagreened surface suggestive of an ostrich-egg. Thickly applied soft ivory glaze of uniform color, showing network of minute crackle. Attributable to the Sung Dynasty. Teakwood stand.

397—TALL IVORY-WHITE VASE

Height, 17¼ inches.

Tapering cylindrical shape with ovoid shoulder and broad neck; light buff-toned paste, without ornamentation, presenting a fluent old-ivory glazing with a network of minute crackle. Sung Dynasty. Teakwood stand.

398—TALL OLD IVORY-WHITE BEAKER

Height, 21½ inches.

Central section in quadrangular form, with shorn corners; spreading base and trumpet neck. The four sides of the center with incised ornament presenting conventional dragon scrolls, the lower section finished with a descending leaf-bordering, and the neck with ascending leaves. Uniformly covered with a deep ivory-white crackled glazing. Sung Dynasty.

BLUE AND WHITE PORCELAINS

400—THREE BLUE AND WHITE BIRD-CAGE UTENSILS

Decoration in cobalt blue on white ground showing delicate peony and vine motifs on two pieces, while the small disk sustains "*fu* lions." Era of Ch'ien-lung (1736-1795).

401—SOFT-PASTE BLUE AND WHITE BIRD-SEED CUP

Of inverted cone shape, the cobalt-blue decoration presenting conventional peony blossoms with foliated stems, under a soft crackled glazing. Era of Yung Ch'êng (1723-1735).

402—SMALL BLUE AND WHITE PORCELAIN COUPE

Globular, with small aperture. Pure white hard-paste porcelain, with cobalt-blue decoration under the glaze presenting a landscape scene, with sages or mandarins and boy attendants. The details include railed terraces, steps and rocky cliffs. Bears mark underneath in six characters, "Ta Ming Chia Ching nien-chih" (1522-1566), but the object may be attributed to the beginning of the XVIIIth century. Has teakwood stand.

403—SMALL BLUE AND WHITE SOFT-PASTE COUPE

Diameter, 3 inches.

Globular, with small aperture, the cobalt-blue decoration presenting a pair of five-clawed dragons in quest of the flaming orb, midst cloud patches. One of the dragons is rising from the sea. Soft-toned glazing with slight crackle. Era of Yung Ch'êng. Has teakwood stand.

404—DECORATED LAPIS-BLUE SEAL COLOR-BOX

Diameter, 2¾ inches.

Low circular form. Fine Ta Ch'ing porcelain, decoration showing a dragon amid clouds in white reserve, against a lapis-blue ground under brilliant glazing. Six-character Ming mark (apocryphal). Attributable to the K'ang-hsi period. Teakwood stand.

405—BLUE AND WHITE SOFT-PASTE PORCELAIN VASE

Height, 7 inches.

Ovated shape, with slender neck and curved dragon-head handles, the cobalt-blue decoration presenting rampant dragons and phœnixes, with base and neck borders of varied form. On the rim a fret pattern, enclosing six-character mark: "Ta Ming Hsüan Tê nien-chih." Teakwood stand.

406—BLUE AND WHITE PORCELAIN BOTTLE WITH SLENDER NECK

Height, 7½ inches.

Fine white porcelain with deep cobalt-blue painting under the pellucid glaze, presenting a series of three formally posed lotus flowers amidst scrolling foliations. Neck finished by a palmation bordering. Six-character mark, "Ta Ming Ch'êng Hua nien-chih," but ascribed to the period of K'ang-hsi. Has teakwood stand.

407—*SOFT-PASTE BLUE AND WHITE VASE*

Height, 8 inches.

Graceful ovated form with receding neck and base. Cobalt-blue decoration, under a delicately crackled glaze, presenting three sages seated under a pine tree, occupied over a game of chess. Early XVIIIth century. Has teakwood stand.

408—BLUE AND WHITE PORCELAIN BOTTLE

Height, 8¾ inches.

Globular body with bulbous middle section and slender neck. K'ang-hsi porcelain of massive quality presenting varied symbolical emblems, among which appear precious vessels, tripods and vases, musical instruments, fans, books and lotus flowers, rendered in deep cobalt-blue; neck includes a lotus-leaf bordering. Era of K'ang-hsi (1662-1722). Teakwood stand.

409—BLUE AND WHITE OVOID VASE WITH SHORT NECK

Height, 7½ inches.

Pure white K'ang-hsi porcelain, sustaining phœnix and dragon decoration, with the jewel of omnipotence and cloud patches. Bears seal mark of felicitous character. Era of K'ang-hsi. Has stand.

410—SMALL BLUE AND WHITE CLUB-SHAPED VASE

Height, 8 inches.

Cylindrical body, with short straight neck. Fine white porcelain, with a deep cobalt-blue landscape subject under the glaze, presenting mountains, a lake with boatmen, and habitations; the details including pine trees, bamboo and birds. The neck with vermiculate and escalloped border. Era of K'ang-hsi. Has teakwood stand.

411—TALL BLUE AND WHITE BEAKER-SHAPED VASE

Height, 18¼ inches.

With slightly spreading base and flaring, flanged neck. Fine white porcelain with cobalt-blue decoration in landscape and floral panels of oval and quadrilateral form. Ground filled with blue dotting, to suggest the grain pattern. Lanceolated and fret bordering at neck. Bears ring mark; ascribed to the era of K'ang-hsi.

412—BLUE AND WHITE BEAKER

Height, 18 inches.

In form and decoration matching the preceding, but the blue of lighter tone. Era of K'ang-hsi (1662-1722). Teakwood stand.

413—LARGE BLUE AND WHITE VASE

Height, 17 inches.

Ovoid with narrow neck and spreading base. Clear white porcelain presenting *mei-hua* trees raised and picked out in deep cobalt-blue, with white blossoms set off by blue clouding under the glaze. The design in free rendering with the spreading branches of the tree encircling the body. The neck has narrow borderings, and twigs of the plum tree in blue on the white ground. Double ring mark. Made era of K'ang-hsi (1662-1722). Teakwood stand.

414—TALL BLUE AND WHITE BEAKER

Height, 17 inches.

Fine white texture with cobalt-blue decoration showing the phœnix and *ch'i-lin* midst scrolling and floral motifs on the neck, and the lower body displaying a symmetrical blue scroll motif including chrysanthemums and storks. Era of K'ang-hsi (1662-1722). Teakwood stand.

415—TALL BLUE AND WHITE VASE

Height, 19¼ inches.

Ovoid with narrowed neck and slightly spreading base. Fine white porcelain with cobalt-blue decoration of mountains and rocky ledges, fishermen in a boat and other figures, while flocks of birds appear near the shoulder. A conventional narrow bordering finishes the neck. Ring mark under the foot. Attributable to the era of K'ang-hsi. Teakwood stand.

416—LARGE BLUE AND WHITE PALACE VASE

Height, 28 inches.

Unique baluster-shape with small, bulbous section above shoulder, and flaring neck. Clear white porcelain with cobalt-blue painting of lustrous quality under a perfect glaze. The design includes floral medallions and jardinière motifs, with conventional flowering scrolls: shoulder and base with slightly raised lanceolated bordering, bearing lotus flower and arabesque details. The neck, with similar decoration, includes floral medallions and jardinière motifs, completed by a floral rim band. On the foot, double ring mark enclosing a sacred fungus (*ling chih*). Era of K'ang-hsi (1662-1722). Teakwood stand.

417—REMARKABLE TALL BLUE AND WHITE BEAKER

Height, 30¼ inches.

Tall oviform body with trumpet neck. Clear white K'ang-hsi porcelain with a brilliant cobalt-blue landscape and figure subject, painted under the glaze, showing a garden occupied by numerous ladies engaged in varied occupations, including music, painting and chess, and with a floral adornment. Neck surrounded by borders of children with a female attendant. Without mark. Period of K'ang-hsi (1662-1722). Teakwood stand.

(Illustrated.)

417

418—PAIR LARGE BLUE AND WHITE MING JARS WITH COVERS

Height, 13¾ inches; diameter, 15 inches.

Massive oviform with short neck. Dense Ming porcelain with decoration in deep Mohammedan blue, the central motif being a garden scene with numerous boys at play, attended by their tutor who is seated at a table. The accessories include palm trees and cloud forms; the bordering at the shoulder consists of a swastika fret pattern, interrupted by four floral vignettes, and that at the base of palmations. Each bears six-character mark of the Ming Dynasty, and each has hat-shaped teakwood cover, carved in openwork. Era of Chia Ching (1522-1566). Teakwood stand.

419—SMALL TURQUOISE-BLUE BOTTLE

Height, 3 inches.

Pear shape with slender neck. Monochrome glaze in turquoise color of even quality. Era of Yung Ch'êng. With stand.

420—SMALL MIRROR-BLACK BOTTLE

Height, 3⅛ inches.

Pear shape with slender neck, presenting the so-called "mirror black" glaze of even color and brilliancy. Era of Yung Ch'êng (1723-1735). Teakwood stand.

421—SMALL LEAF-SHAPED TRAY

Length, 3¾ inches.

Natural repand form, showing buckled edges, with a second and smaller leaf near the stem. Fine Ta Ch'ing porcelain, the interior invested with a pale green glazing, the underside glazed in white with a greenish tinge. Incised hall mark. Era of Ch'ien-lung (1736-1795). Has carved teakwood stand representing tree boughs.

422—SMALL METALLIC SOUFFLÉ VASE

Height, 3 inches.

Perfect ovoid shape with small aperture. Early Ta Ch'ing porcelain with deep copper-red glaze showing the so-called iron-rust flecking. Early XVIIIth century. Ta Ch'ing Dynasty. Teakwood stand.

423—FLAMBÉ BOTTLE

Height, 6 inches.

Graceful ovoid shape with slender neck; semi-kaolinic stoneware, coated with a blended lapis-blue and deep turquoise-colored glazing, of the *flambé* variety. Era of Yung Ch'êng. Has teakwood stand.

424—MONOCHROME BOTTLE

Height, 6 inches.

Double-gourd shape, cabinet size. Rare Ta Ch'ing porcelain, presenting a uniform translucent starch-blue (*tien lan*) glaze of delicate quality. Era of Yung Ch'êng (1723-1735). Teakwood stand.

425—RARE METALLIC SOUFFLÉ BOTTLE

Height, 6¼ inches.

Biberon shape (*mei p'ing*), cabinet size. Early Ta Ch'ing porcelain presenting a uniform metallic *soufflé* speckling of silver-like grains upon the copper-red ground-glaze. The neck is distinguished by a brownish-red glazing, both without and within, while the glaze underneath the foot is of brown and grayish tones. Early Ch'ien-lung. Teakwood stand.

426—SMALL CAMELLIA-LEAF GREEN BOTTLE

Height, 5¼ inches.

Pear-shaped with slender neck; early Ta Ch'ing porcelain invested with a so-called camellia-leaf green glazing which shows the usual small crackle, together with iridescence. Era of K'ang-hsi (1662-1722). Teakwood stand.

427—SMALL CORAL-RED BOTTLE

Height, 5½ inches.

Graceful biberon form of cabinet size and fine texture. Ta Ch'ing porcelain, with a coral-red glaze of even quality, distinguished by a slight linear marking across the center. Sunken circular white glazed panel within the unglazed foot. Era of K'ang-hsi (**1662-1722**).

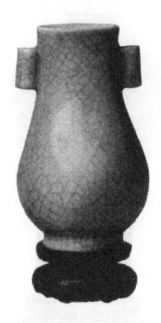

428—SMALL HANGING VASE

Height, 5½ inches.

Oviform body with receding neck sustaining tubular handles; so-called "green Lang porcelain," with an apple-green glaze of rare quality, and a giant crackle. Interior of neck coated with whitish-toned céladon glazing with crackle; the foot in apple-green glaze with the usual brown rim. Attributable to the XVIIth century (close of the Ming Dynasty, or early K'ang-hsi). Has teakwood stand.

429—MONOCHROME BOTTLE

Height, 8¼ inches.

Graceful oviform body, with slender neck. Fine Ta Ch'ing porcelain invested with a delicate slate-blue glaze of even translucent quality. Unglazed biscuit foot. Era of Yung Ch'êng (1723-1735).

430—WHITE AND CORAL-RED DECORATED VASE

Height, 7 inches.

Ovoid body with low, slightly spreading neck and narrow foot. Pure white Ta Ch'ing porcelain with coral-red decoration displaying a lotus flower and pond motif, beautifully rendered in coral tones. Underneath the foot a turquoise glaze, and seal mark, "Made era of Ch'ien-lung," the turquoise glaze being repeated on the interior of the neck. Teakwood stand.

431—DARK METALLIC SOUFFLÉ BOTTLE

Height, 7 inches.

Double-gourd shape, cabinet size; early Ta Ch'ing porcelain coated with a dark copper-brown ground color sustaining closely speckled steel-like particles. Termed iron-rust glaze, or *tieh hsui hua* by the Chinese. Early Ch'ien-lung (1736-1795). Teakwood stand.

432—UNIQUE CRACKLED VASE

Height, 6½ inches.

Graceful biberon shape, of cabinet size; dense white paste invested with a gray-blue glaze of translucent quality and brown crackle. Sunken panel underneath foot showing a céladon glaze. Era of K'ang-hsi (1662-1722). Teakwood stand.

433—CLAIR-DE-LUNE PLATE

Diameter, 7½ inches.

Shallow round form of semi-kaolinic stoneware covered with an opaque *clair-de-lune* glaze. Under side shows three segger marks from the kiln. Yuan Dynasty.

434—SMALL APPLE-GREEN JAR

Height, 5⅝ inches.

Ovoid shape, so-called "green Lang porcelain"; fine apple-green glaze of even color with crackle and an iridescent quality. Interior in céladon glazing with crackle, the foot underneath showing the same glaze; the rim also. Close of the Ming Dynasty. With teakwood stand.

435—MONOCHROME BOTTLE

Height, 8¾ inches.

Pear-shape with tubular neck. Ch'ien-lung porcelain, presenting a rare light lemon-yellow glaze, with pear-skin texture. Fine cabinet example. Ta Ch'ing Dynasty. Teakwood stand.

436—BLUE PORCELAIN BOTTLE

Height, 7½ inches.

Ovoid shape with small neck, suggesting a *mei p'ing* form. White Ta Ch'ing porcelain with monochrome glaze of starch-blue tone. Era of Ch'ien-lung (1736-1795). Teakwood stand.

437—DECORATED BOTTLE

Height, 8¼ inches.

Pear-shape with full neck. Fine white Ta Ch'ing porcelain; decoration presenting a lotus flower motif in peach-color, with moss-green speckling; rich body glaze of peculiar perfection and brilliance. Early K'ang-hsi (1662-1722). Ta Ch'ing Dynasty. Teakwood stand.

438—BRILLIANT SAPPHIRE-BLUE BOTTLE

Height, 8¼ inches.

Globular body with tubular neck. Early Ta Ch'ing porcelain of hard texture, covered with a rare sapphire-blue glaze of even color and brilliancy. Foot in biscuit unglazed. Era of K'ang-hsi (1662-1722). Teakwood stand.

439—RARE IRON-RUST SOUFFLÉ VASE

Height, 9 inches.

Oviform with small neck. Ch'ien-lung porcelain with dark copper-brown ground and metallic *soufflé* glaze, with purplish red-flecking. Early XVIIIth century. Ta Ch'ing Dynasty. Teakwood stand.

440—ROBIN'S-EGG BLUE FLAMBÉ BOWL

Diameter, 7¾ inches.

Globular form with wide mouth. Ta Ch'ing porcelain presenting the robin's-egg blue glaze with purplish flecking, rendered in scale-like forms, resembling the reversed lotus flower petals. Rare technical achievement. Panel underneath foot with speckled robin's-egg glaze, sustaining impressed four-character mark. Made era of Yung Ch'êng (1723-1735). Has teakwood stand.

441—DEEP LAPIS-BLUE TRIPOD BOWL

Diameter, 8½ inches.

Dense white Ming porcelain, the exterior covered with brilliant lapis-blue glaze, sustaining white "slip" decoration (*pâte sur pâte*) in the form of phœnix-birds, with the symbolic jewel, and interspersed with convoluted cloud patterns. The interior finished with a white glaze. Foot underneath bears mark in four characters (*yü tang chea ke*), "Beautiful vessel of the jade hall," meaning the academy. Ming Dynasty. Fitted with teakwood stand, and a teakwood cover surmounted by an aquamarine quartz ornament.

442—IMPERIAL YELLOW BOTTLE WITH GILT NECK

Height, 9 inches.

Graceful, tapering, amphora shape, the short neck finished in silver-gilt. Ta Ch'ing porcelain with a delicately impressed ornamentation of two imperial dragons rampant, midst nebulæ, under an imperial yellow glaze. Six-character mark on foot in blue: "Ta Ch'ing K'ang-hsi nien-chih." Teakwood stand.

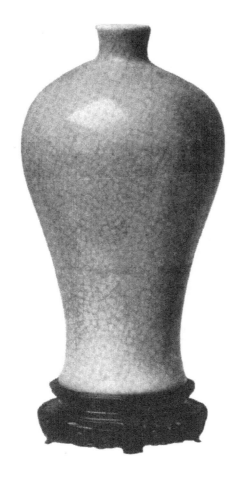

443—APPLE-GREEN BOTTLE

Height, 9 inches.

Biberon shape, so-called "green Lang porcelain" covered with a monochrome green glaze of apple-green hue, showing even crackling with rare quality. XVIIth century. Close of the Ming or early K'ang-hsi period. Carved teakwood stand.

444—APPLE-GREEN JAR

Diameter, 8¾ inches.

Low shallow form, raised upon three small knob-like feet, the exterior presenting a translucent light apple-green glaze, suggesting the color of *fei-ts'ui* jade, with brownish crackle. Interior coated with a crackled céladon glaze; rim reserved in white. Date: XVIIth century (border line of the Ming and Ch'ing Dynasties). Carved teakwood cover with carved jade ornament; tall teakwood stand.

445—LARGE APPLE-GREEN GINGER JAR WITH COVER

Height, 9 inches.

Ovoid shape, the so-called "green Lang porcelain" with translucent apple-green glaze of even quality, including a vitreous speckling and crackle. Color suggesting emerald-green jadeite of light tone. Foot underneath coated with a thin brown glazing. Date: XVIIth century, or border line of the Ming and Ch'ing Dynasties. Has teakwood stand and cover, the latter surmounted by a jade ornament.

SERIES OF RARE PEACHBLOOM OBJECTS

446—LIGHT PEACHBLOOM BIRD-SEED COUPE

Globular form with small annular handle; fine Ch'ing porcelain coated with a light peach-red glaze, with moss-green clouding. Yung Ch'êng (1723-1735).

447—RARE PEACHBLOOM COLOR-BOX

Low rounded form (*yin sê ho*); clear white Ta Ch'ing porcelain. Cover and lower exterior of bowl presenting a beautiful modeling of peach-red tones, with intermediate green speckling. Interior with white glaze which is repeated on the foot. Without mark. Ascribed to the era of K'ang-hsi, of the Ta Ch'ing Dynasty. With stand.

(*Illustrated.*)

448—REMARKABLE PEACHBLOOM BOX

Low rounded form; clear white Ta Ch'ing porcelain. Cover and lower exterior of bowl displaying a rare variety of the peach-red glaze, with beautifully blended tones of moss-green flecking. A rare example of this treasured porcelain. The white-glazed foot with six-character mark in underglaze cobalt-blue: "Ta Ch'ing K'ang-hsi nien-chih" (1662-1722). Teakwood stand.

(*Illustrated.*)

449—RARE PEACHBLOOM WATER COUPE

Low circular form, clear white Ta Ch'ing porcelain; the rounded exterior sustaining a beautifully mottled peach-red glaze, emphasized by a delicate clouding of brilliant moss-green tones. Interior glazed in white, as is the panel underneath, which bears the full six-character mark in fine cobalt-blue: "Ta Ch'ing K'ang-hsi nien-chih" (1662-1722). Tall carved teakwood stand.

(*Illustrated.*)

450—RARE PEACHBLOOM COUPE

Low circular form (*t'ai-po ts'un*), clear white Ta Ch'ing porcelain; the rounded exterior sustaining a beautiful *peau-de-pêche* glaze with light clouding, and including young onion-sprout and delicate mauve-like shading. Interior glazed in white as is the foot, which bears six-character mark in cobalt-blue: "Ta Ch'ing K'ang-hsi nien-chih" (1662-1722). Tall carved teakwood stand.

(*Illustrated.*)

447

448

449

450

452

451—IMPERIAL YELLOW WATER RECEPTACLE

Diameter, 5 inches.

Semi-globular shape with small aperture. Decorated with three dragon crests delicately incised in the paste under an Imperial yellow glaze. Foot bears a six-character mark in black under the yellow glaze: "Ta Ch'ing K'ang-hsi nien-chih (1662-1722). Teakwood stand.

452—PEACHBLOOM WATER RECEPTACLE

Diameter, 5 inches.

Low semi-spherical shape (*shui ch'ing*) with small aperture. Clear white Ta Ch'ing porcelain; incised with three small dragon crests in rounded medallion form delicately rendered under the soft peach-red glaze. Showing beautiful *peau-de-pêche* variations combined with green moss clouding. The foot in white glaze bears six-character mark in cobalt-blue: "Ta Ch'ing K'ang-hsi nien-chih" (1662-1722). Low teakwood stand.

(*Illustrated.*)

453—RARE PEARL-GRAY AMPHORA-SHAPED VASE

Height, 6¼ inches.

Graceful form, fashioned on the lines of the small peachbloom amphoras, and made in the Imperial kilns. Pure white early Ta Ch'ing porcelain covered with a translucent monochrome glaze of pearl gray, called also *claire-de-lune*, a color greatly appreciated in China. Foot with six-character mark: "Ta Ch'ing K'ang-hsi nien-chih" (1662-1722). Tall carved stand.

457

GROUP OF SINGLE-COLOR SPECIMENS

454—SANG-DE-BŒUF COUPE

Diameter, 3 inches.

Low globular form with wide aperture, the exterior showing a rich blending of light and dark ox-blood tones, with a céladon clouding and crackle near the base. Upper rim defined by white glazing and the panel underneath in white, without mark. Date: XVIIth century. Teakwood stand.

455—SANG-DE-BŒUF VASE

Height, 8 inches; diameter, 4 inches.

Pyriform *Lang yao* of hard white texture. Sustaining brilliant red glaze of the rare *sang-de-bœuf* genre, with ruby-like blending, including characteristic mottled clod-like blending, together with céladon zones at the base. (Slightly cracked and mended.) Date: XVIIth century, or border line of the Ming and Ch'ing Dynasties. Teakwood stand.

456—LARGE SANG-DE-BŒUF VASE .

Height, 15¼ inches; diameter, 8½ inches.

Fine rounded baluster-form with short neck and silver-gilt mounting on upper rim. Dense *Lang yao* of typical quality and full red color presenting a deep ox-blood glaze with clotted blending, merging into brilliant ruby-like tones toward the base, with the liquescent red glaze clearly defined and finishing at the lower rim. Underneath foot sustains crackled white glaze. Date: XVIIth century. Teakwood cover and stand, former including jade ornament mounting.

457—TALL SANG-DE-BŒUF BOTTLE

Height, 17 inches.

Globular body and long tapering neck. Dense *Lang yao* coated with the typical ox-blood glaze, including deep tones, with clouding, and finishing at the base in characteristic perfection. Foot showing rice-colored crackle. Date: XVIIth century. Teakwood stand.

(Illustrated.)

458—SMALL SANG-DE-BŒUF BOTTLE

Height, 5¼ inches.

Pear-shape with tall tubular receding neck; dense *Lang yao* coated with the *sang-de-bœuf* glaze and presenting characteristic clotting of deeper tone. Panel underneath with white glaze. Date: XVIIth century. Teakwood stand.

459—*RARE SANG-DE-BŒUF VASE*

Height, 6½ inches.

Graceful biberon form (*mei p'ing*). *Lang-yao* of dense white quality; cabinet size. Coated with a brilliant red glaze which displays the characteristic tones only found in the famed red Lang porcelains, the coloring passing from translucent ruby tones to the deeper ox-blood clotting. Foot in a rice-colored crackle glaze. Date: XVIIth century. Teakwood stand.

460—LARGE CÉLADON AND RUBY-RED BOTTLE

Height, 15½ inches.

Typical shape, with round thick-set body and broad cylindrical neck. Dense kaolinic porcelain invested with a rich ruby-red glaze on the shoulder and above the foot, on a ground of crackled céladon. Foot and interior of neck with white crackle glaze. Era of K'ang-hsi (1662-1722). Teakwood stand.

(Illustrated.)

461—LARGE SANG-DE-BŒUF VASE

Height, 17 inches.

Tall baluster-form; dense kaolinic paste, invested with a remarkably brilliant glaze of the ox-blood variety. Lower rim shows well-defined marginal line at the ending of the flowing glaze. Foot with a rice-color glaze with crackle, which also appears on the interior of the neck. Date: XVIIth century. Teakwood stand.

(Illustrated.)

462—LARGE SANG-DE-BŒUF VASE

Height, 18 inches.

Tall ovoid form with flaring neck and spreading foot. Invested with a typical *sang-de-bœuf* glaze of rare perfection, with interesting variations and céladon tints. Wonderful technical precision is shown at the base, in the well-defined limit of the glaze. Date: XVIIth century. Teakwood stand.

463—MYRTLE-GREEN TRIPOD BOWL

Diameter, 9¾ inches.

Low circular body with three fungiform feet. Semi-kaolinic stoneware with simple ornamentation; exterior presenting two rows of nodular bossing around the upper and lower rims. Coated with brilliant myrtle green glazing, both exterior and interior showing a blending of olive tones. Ming Dynasty. Teakwood stand.

460

461

464—CLAIR-DE-LUNE TRIPOD BOWL

Diameter, 10¼ inches.

Low circular shape, raised upon three fungiform feet; dense semi-kaolinic stoneware, with simple ornamentation presenting two rows of nodular bossing; copied from ancient sacrificial bronzes. Interior and exterior uniformly glazed in mottled-blue (*clair-de-lune*) glazing, showing olive-color in parts of the ornament. Mark with numeral of the kiln, 1. Early Ming Dynasty.

465—LARGE IMPERIAL PLATE

Diameter, 12½ inches.

Deep shape; the interior with a medallion presenting a pair of dragons midst cloud forms, in pursuit of the effulgent jewel, delicately etched, with a floral bordering and chrysanthemum, lotus and peony flowers. The reverse sustains four dragons pursuing the jewel. Coated with a brilliant Imperial yellow glaze. White foot with six-character mark in blue. Era of Ch'ien-lung. Teakwood stand with carved and pierced jade panel.

466—LARGE IMPERIAL YELLOW BOWL

Diameter, 15 inches.

Monochrome glaze. Conventional form with rounded sides. Sonorous white porcelain, coated with a rich yellow (*huang sê*) glazing of translucent quality and even color. White panel underneath bears six-character mark in blue: "Ta Ming Chia Ching nien-chih" (1522-1566). Teakwood stand.

467—LARGE WHITE BIBERON-SHAPED BOTTLE

Height, 14 inches.

Termed *mei p'ing* by the Chinese, showing a small neck, intended to hold a single sprig of plum blossoms. Hard-paste white porcelain with raised ornamentation presenting a pair of dragons amid clouds in quest of the jewel of omnipotence. Base showing a swirling wave motif. Era of Ch'ing-lung (1736-1795). With teakwood stand.

468—LARGE MIRROR-BLACK VASE

Height, 14 inches.

Tall biberon-shape (*mei p'ing*) with small neck and graceful contour. Ta Ch'ing porcelain, presenting a *wu liang hei* or "mirror-black" glaze, of iridescent quality and showing flecking in olive-brown and blue tones. Era of K'ang-hsi (1662-1722). Teakwood stand.

469—LARGE GALLIPOT

Height, 14 inches.

Ta Ch'ing porcelain with purplish-blue glaze and orange peel surface. Era of Chia-Ch'ing (1796-1820). Teakwood stand.

470

471

470—TALL POWDER-BLUE CLUB-SHAPED VASE

Height, 18¼ inches.

Cylindrical shape, with sloping shoulder, tubular neck and flanged lip; K'ang-hsi porcelain coated with a brilliant blue *soufflé* glaze, overlaid with an intricate gold decoration in two large panels of landscape subjects, and small round and leaf-shaped medallions which enclose art objects and Buddhistic lions, dragons, phœnixes and chrysanthemums on a ground of vermiculate design. Shoulder with brocaded bordering, including small medallions; neck encircled by varied conventional bands. Without mark. Ascribable to the era of K'ang-hsi. Teakwood stand.

(*Illustrated.*)

471—TALL POWDER-BLUE CLUB-SHAPED VASE

Height, 18¼ inches.

Cylindrical form with square shoulder, tubular neck and flanged lip; early Ta Ch'ing porcelain invested with a brilliant powder-blue *soufflé* glaze overlaid with intricate gold painting in two large vertical panels that sustain landscape and figure subjects with agricultural details. The shoulder surrounded by a diapered band, including vignettes with emblems, while the neck sustains treasured art objects known as the "hundred antiques." Without mark; ascribable to the era of K'ang-hsi. Ta Ch'ing Dynasty. Has stand.

(*Illustrated.*)

472—REMARKABLE TALL PEACOCK-BLUE BOTTLE

Height, 28¼ inches; diameter, 9¾ inches.

Slender biberon shape with small neck. Ta Ch'ing porcelain; coated in monochrome peacock-blue glaze (*Kung Chou lü*) invested with the so-called "shad-roe" (*truité*) crackle, showing uniform and rare quality. Era of K'ang-hsi (1662-1722). Teakwood stand.

473—LARGE FAMILLE-VERTE VASE

Height, 18¾ inches; diameter, 8½ inches.

Graceful baluster-form. Fine white texture K'ang-hsi porcelain, decorated in various enameled colors. The design presents a landscape subject with warriors, including horsemen and a mythical being who rides upon the fabled *ch'i-lin*. The details include habitations, mountain peaks, and symbolical trees, delicately rendered in the varied opaque and translucent colors with the green tones dominant. Without mark. Attributable to the era of K'ang-hsi (1662-1722). With teakwood stand.

474—TALL FAMILLE-VERTE VASE

Height, 18¾ inches.

Slender oviform with short and wide neck; clear white porcelain with seven-color decoration of a ceremonial scene with ladies of the court and their attendants receiving personages of distinction, a pavilion with a tessellated marble floor, and a table on which appear dishes and candlesticks. A continuation of the panoramic scene shows the interior of a smaller pavilion where attendants are refreshing themselves. The painting is completed by tall palm and pine trees, open rockeries, terraces and cloud patches. Without mark. Ascribable to the era of K'ang-hsi (1662-1722). Teakwood stand.

475—IMPORTANT LARGE CÉLADON VASE

Height, 24½ inches; diameter, 12 inches.

Tall oviform body with trumpet neck. Heavy Ming (*Lung Ch'uan yao*) porcelain, with relief and incised embellishment including foliations. The middle section showing a band with floral vines, the base surrounded by fluting, and the neck by ascending leafage intersected by horizontal ribbing. Invested with an opaque céladon glaze of rare quality. Massive foot with ferruginous (iron-red) rim. Ta Ming Dynasty. Teakwood stand.

476—LARGE MING CÉLADON COUPE

Height, 6½ inches; diameter, 19 inches.

Shallow rounded shape; dense ferruginous porcelain, supported upon three teakwood feet. Exterior embellishment, in low relief, presenting lotus flowers with scrolling stems and foliation, flanked by rosette-like bossing above and below, with céladon glaze of iridescent quality. The interior is partly glazed, the center being left in the biscuit state which is to be seen again underneath. Ming Dynasty. Carved teakwood cover with jade ornament, and carved teakwood stand.

477—LARGE DECORATED LAPIS-BLUE JAR

Height, 12¾ inches; diameter, 13¼ inches.

Wide oviform with low, contracted neck. Sonorous Ming porcelain presenting a deep lapis-blue ground, with a white slip decoration in low relief in pinkish-coral and ivory-white tones. Varied borderings showing lions disporting with the brocaded ball, a larger lion appearing on one side with a character "Wang" (meaning king) on the forehead. Foot in unglazed paste. Ming Dynasty. Carved teakwood hat-shaped cover and stand, the former surmounted by jade knob.

(Illustrated.)

478—*TWO LARGE MING TURQUOISE VASES*

Height, 20¼ inches.

Tall oviform shape with flaring neck and bulging shoulder, tapering downward to base. Ming pottery; coated with blended turquoise- and peacock-blue glaze, showing strong marking of *truité* crackle. Ming Dynasty. With stands.

(*Illustrated.*)

479—*TURQUOISE POTTERY BEAKER*

Height, 14 inches; diameter, 6 inches.

Globular center section with radial dentilations and dragon crests posed midst impressed ground of diapering, in geometric form. Spreading base sustaining broad descending leaf bordering, while the trumpet- shaped neck presents a bordering of ascending leafage. Coated in monochrome turquoise-colored glaze. Slight mending at neck. Ming Dynasty. Teakwood stand.

480—*TURQUOISE POTTERY BEAKER*

Height, 16½ inches; diameter, 7 inches.

Similar shape and glazing; made after ancient bronze prototype of the Chou period during the Ming Dynasty. Teakwood stand.

481—*MING POTTERY TRIPOD INCENSE BURNER*

Height, 10¼ inches; diameter, 8 inches.

Globular shape, with flanged neck, and raised on three tapering feet. Elaborate handles modeled in dragon and fungus forms; the body, with varied bordering, sustains an impressed diapering, or so- called grain pattern. Ming pottery, copied from ancient bronzes; coated in monochrome turquoise-blue glaze. Original cover with relief bordering sustaining the eight (*pa-kua*) symbols of broken and unbroken lines. The top is surmounted by a grotesque lion. Foot unerneath bears impressed seal mark, "Chu ye" (one of the classics of Confucius); made after a Chou bronze. Ming Dynasty. Teakwood stand.

482—TEMPLE INCENSE BURNER WITH COVER

Height, 14¾ inches with cover; width, 8 inches.

Oblong shape, with four tubular legs, and arched rim handles. Ming pottery, fashioned after an ancient (*Ting*) bronze sacrificial vessel. Corners sustaining lateral dentated ridges, while the sides, including small angular convoluted scrolled plaquettes, are impressed with nodular millet-like bossing. Surmounted by a grotesque lion, the cover is decorated with raised foliation and crest-like ornaments. Vessel and cover uniformly coated in turquoise-blue glaze, showing slight earthy incrustations in crevices. Teakwood stand.

483—ANOTHER TEMPLE INCENSE BURNER WITH COVER

Matching the preceding in both design and size, the turquoise-blue glazing including brownish clouding. Ming Dynasty.

484—TWO SAPPHIRE-BLUE CUT-GLASS VASES

Height, 18½ inches; diameter of rim, 10 inches.

In beaker form with trumpet-lip, narrow stem and octagonal base. Fashioned with middle section in ovoidal shape, and upper and lower in octagonal form. European make.

485—TWO TALL SAPPHIRE-BLUE CUT-GLASS VASES

Height, 23¼ inches; diameter, 14 inches.

Urn shape, with square base; cut in three sections, the middle showing a ribbed body, and the upper rim an escalloped or gadroon bordering form. European make. Matching the preceding in color. Date: XIXth century.

486—GRAY FÊN TING YAO COUPE WITH COVER

Height, 4½ inches.

Globular form; decoration showing recurrent grayish-toned bands that enclose small hairline segments under the glaze. Attributable to the close of the Sung Dynasty. Teakwood stand.

478

487—PAIR OF DECORATED POTTERY VASES

Height, 10 inches; diameter, 4 inches.

Quadrilateral shape with swelling body, contracted neck with expanded square lip, and pyramidal base. Small monster-head handles on two sides of the neck. Emerald-green ground, relieved by yellow dragons that rise from the sea and yellow carp rising from purple and white waves. Base, with like green ground, displays running horses, picked out in yellow under the glaze. Date: XVIIth century, border line of the Ta Ming and Ta Ch'ing Dynasties. Has teakwood stand.

488—DECORATED IVORY-WHITE VASE

Height, 12¾ inches.

Tall biberon (*mei-p'ing*) shape with tapering contour and narrow flaring neck; incised decoration of a peony flower motif freely rendered, with stems and foliations. Covered with a mellowed old-ivory glaze. Probably made toward the close of the Sung Dynasty. Teakwood stand.

489—MING SHRINE GROUP

Height, 14 inches; width, 7¼ inches.

Representing Kwan-yin (Avalokites-vara), the compassionate hearer of prayers, accompanied by a small boy, seated on a rocky elevation guarded by a dragon. The divinity is clad in ancient form, wears a necklace and tiara, and is shown with halo or nimbus. The right hand rests upon the raised knee, close to which appears a parrot. Coated with a deep ivory-white glaze which in parts is relieved by pale russet-red and dark brown tones. Ming Dynasty.

490—DECORATED MING JARDINIÈRE

Height, 14 inches; diameter, 12½ inches.

Garden-seat of dense, semi-kaolinic stoneware, fitted with a copper interior. Wide mid-band of pierced work, glazed in turquoise, deep blue, yellow and lavender-brown, and bearing two rudimentary mask-like handles, Buddhistic emblems, winged dragons, rock and wave designs. Upper and lower borders in dark lapis-blue with nodular turquoise bossing; the lower band including horses and wave designs in yellow, green and turquoise-blue tones. Era of Chêng Tê (1506-1622). Ming Dynasty.

491—DECORATED MING JARDINIÈRE

Height, 14¼ inches; diameter, 13 inches.

Garden-seat of dense semi-kaolinic stoneware, with a copper interior. The embellishment includes two rudimentary, mask-like handles on the wide central band, which is glazed in turquoise-blue and reveals cranes and lotus flower motifs in aubergine and yellow, with a modicum of floral forms in white reserve. Upper and lower bands of solid dark lapis-blue glazing, with rows of nodular bossing. Chêng Tê period of the Ming Dynasty.

492—LARGE WHITE SUNG PLANT JAR

Height, 17½ inches; diameter, 26 inches.

Broad semi-globular shape. Massive *Fên-Ting yao*; fashioned with broad rim and two small grotesque masks at the sides suggesting handles, the exterior presenting border of undulating wave-like lines. Slightly raised, under the ivory-white glazing and border forms. Sung Dynasty.

493—LARGE BLUE AND WHITE PORCELAIN PLANT JAR

Height, 22½ inches; diameter, 26½ inches.

Cylindrical form with slight taper. Sonorous Ta Ch'ing porcelain of massive form, with cobalt-blue decoration under the glaze presenting numerous dragons and cloud forms on a white ground. Base encircled by a wave pattern and rim by a border enclosing lotus flowers and scrolls. Date: XVIIIth century. Ta Ch'ing Dynasty. Tall teakwood stand.

494—LARGE PEACOCK-BLUE PLANT JAR

Height, 22 inches; diameter, 29 inches.

Slightly bulging cylindrical form, dense Ming paste; massive proportions. Covered with deep peacock-blue glaze, slightly clouded and covered with a network of crackle. It is possible that this jar was formerly used to hold fish in the garden. Ming Dynasty. Has teakwood stand.

495—PAIR OF LARGE WHITE MARBLE LIONS

Height, 12 inches; width, 17½ inches.

Sculptured in recumbent form on low square bases, as architectural accessories, from white marble showing dark stains and weathering.

496—PAIR OF LARGE MING LIONS

Height, 32 inches; width, 15 inches; depth, 20 inches.

Strongly modeled in conventional form, seated upon their haunches; heads turned to right and left. One holds the symbolical sphere under its forepaws, and the other is grouped with its cub. Glazed in deep turquoise, in parts relieved by dark purple. Era Wan Li (1573-1619). Ming Dynasty.

(Illustrated.)

497—GRAND TEMPLE INCENSE BURNER

Height of incense burner with pottery stand, 40 inches.
Total height, 55 inches; width, 33 inches.

Quadrangular shape, with boldly modeled embellishment, including two large upstanding handles enriched by relief figures, and bearing long incised inscriptions of dedication. Supported by four ornately fashioned legs, the body includes dragon forms, together with lotus and orchid blossoms in free relief, is raised on a pottery socle with open top (used for heating purposes), exterior showing sunken panel forms with angular corners which bear human figures. The glazing in three colors, including orange-yellow, turquoise-blue and emerald-green with a medium of dark aubergine. Cover, of carved and gilt teakwood, surmounted by a pottery lion group, glazed to match the vessel. Ming Dynasty. With teakwood stand.

498

In the form of a temple, with double tilted roof and bronze finial. Dense Ming pottery. On a columnar pedestal of stone. Ming Dynasty.

(*Illustrated.*)

CHINESE PAINTINGS ON SILK, OF THE SUNG, YUAN AND MING DYNASTIES

MOUNTED WITH ANCIENT SILK AND GOLD BROCADE, KAKEMONO SCROLL FASHION

500—*SMALL CHINESE PAINTING*

Height, 9¼ inches; length, 10¼ inches.

Square panel with delicately painted *ai-lu* (fish), on golden-brown silk; the fish gracefully leaping or circulating under water midst aquatic plants and lotus flowers. Light reseda and gold brocaded framing. Sung Dynasty.

501—*SMALL CHINESE PAINTING*

Height, 10 inches; length, 10½ inches.

Rounded panel showing sparrows with bamboo and boughs of the plum tree, beautifully rendered in soft colors and with great fidelity, on golden-brown silk. Bears seals of former owners. Mounted with old gold and yellow brocaded framing. Sung Dynasty.

502—PEACOCK AND PEONY FLOWER PANEL

Height, 57½ inches; width, 29 inches.

The painting, on soft old brown silk, representing a peacock under a large flowering peony tree (indicating springtime), the blossoms of the peony showing delicate mauve-like tints with the white. The symbolism is augmented by hovering butterflies. Probably painted by Lu Ki. Era of Wan Li (1573-1619), Ming Dynasty. Framed in natural wood.

503—ANOTHER PEACOCK AND PEONY PANEL

Pendant to preceding, including a peacock and butterfly midst flowering peony trees. Same size, with similar natural-wood frame.

504—LANDSCAPE WITH FIGURES

Height of painting, 39 inches; width, 37 inches.
With silk and gold brocade mounting, 80 inches and 46 inches, respectively.

An idealized Chinese landscape scene, with terraces, pavilions and numerous figures, painted in soft colors on old brown-toned silk. Details include delicately painted pine and willow trees, with picturesque rocky cliffs and distant pine-clad hills. The painting bears an inscription with signature. Ming Dynasty.

505—TWO FIGURES

Painting: Height, 51 inches; width, 32 inches.
With gold brocade mounting, 88 inches and 39 inches.

This painting, rendered with bold strokes, subtle lines and soft colors, on old brown-toned silk, presents a bearded poet—probably Li Peh (or Tai Peh) of the T'ang Dynasty, one of the most celebrated among the Chinese poets. He is clad in a costume of the VIIIth century, and is being led by a young man who bears a lantern. Ming Dynasty.

506—TWO MOUNTED CHINESE PORTRAITS (KAKEMONO)

Painting: Height, 54½ inches; width, 34½ inches.
With brocade mounting, 94 and 40 inches, respectively.

Representing an emperor and empress of ancient times, obviously painted from life, and with great attention to detail of the features. Unsigned by the artist in deference to the exalted rank of his sitters.

(Illustrated.)

507—GREEN HILLS AND NOBLE HOMES

Panel: Height, 56 inches; width, 51 inches.
With gold brocade mounting, 93 inches and 62 inches, respectively.

A landscape of springtime about a noble's country residence midst lofty hills. Numerous pavilions of harmonious architecture are seen in part through the tall pine, palm and magnolia trees. The foreground, which is intersected by a stone wall, presents picturesque rocks and green-clad hills, while green mountains rise in the distance. Typical idealized style of the Ming Dynasty.

508—BIRD AND FLOWER PANEL

Height, 59 inches; width, 19½ inches.
With brocaded silk mounting, 91 inches and 25 inches.

Presenting an egret amid peony flowers, with beautiful foliation, and an intermingling of aster blossoms; rendered in soft colors on a deep tan-toned silk. Bears signature. Ming Dynasty.

509—BIRDS AND TREES

Height of painting, 52 inches; width, 36 inches.
With green and gold brocade mounting, 102 inches and 43 inches.

Representing peacocks in a bamboo grove, together with magpies. Flowers are growing in the foreground, midst rocks, and in the distance is a small stream. Rendered with freedom and harmony on soft old brown silk. Attributable to Lin Liang (XVth century), Ming Dynasty.

510—MOUNTED PANEL WITH LANDSCAPE AND HORSES

Painting: Height, 62 inches; width, 43½ inches.
With blue and gold brocade mounting: Height, 106 inches; width, 50 inches.

Representing two tethered Tengut horses, one white, the other black. The latter is reaching up after a twig of a tree. Characteristic rendering in the style of Chao Meng-fu (*tzu-ang;* XIIIth century). Yuan Dynasty.

511—BUDDHISTIC PAINTING IN COLORS ON BROWN SILK

Height of painting, 63 inches; width, 37½ inches.
With gold brocade mounting, 100 inches and 45½ inches, respectively.

Presenting the Infernal Tribune, with one of the chief regents of Hades, Yen-Mo (Yama Raja), in rich attire, enthroned, with a green halo and attended by maze bearers and the two principal assessors or witnesses with tablets of record. The rendering showing unusual dignity and force, with minute detail. Unsigned; attributable to the Ming Dynasty.

512—PORTRAIT OF A CHINESE NOBLE SCHOLAR AND LADY

Height, 63 inches; width, 41 inches.
With brocaded mounting; Height, 104 inches; width, 48 inches.

Seated together near a table, upon which appear books, a musical instrument and a vase of flowers. Formal, but remarkable example of the Ming Dynasty. Evidently drawn from life; sufficient chiaroscuro is introduced to reproduce the characteristics of strong features. Signed: Tang Yin. Date: About 1500. Period of Chêng Tê. Ming Dynasty.

513—LANDSCAPE WITH FIGURES

Height, 64 inches; width, 34 inches.
With gold and olive green brocade framing, 108 and 45 inches, respectively.

Executed in soft colors on a brown-toned silk. The painting represents a group of five scholars seated in a garden, interested in a game of chess, while their attendants are occupied in serving tea. Accessories include a lotus pond, terrace and a flower vase.

514—CHINESE PAINTING ON SILK (KAKEMONO)

Painting: Height, 65 inches; width, 37 inches.
With blue and gold brocaded mounting: Height, 108 inches; width, 45 inches.

Representing nine white egrets with willow and peony trees, asters and other blossoms. The nine birds are rendered in various positions, representing the "nine thoughts," according to the Chinese expression. Assumably by Liang Chi, who flourished during the XVth century. Sung Dynasty.

515—GARDEN SCENE WITH NUMEROUS FIGURES

Painting: Height, 66 inches; width, 28½ inches.
With gold brocade mounting, 99 inches and 35 inches, respectively.

· The painting, in soft colors on brownish-toned silk, including a high official surrounded by attendants and children. A terraced elevation depicts two sages, assumably Lao-Tsze and Confucius, discoursing over the *yang* and *yin* emblem, which has attracted three youths. Attributable to a master of the XVth century. Ming Dynasty.

516—MOUNTAINOUS LANDSCAPE

Height of painting, 66 inches; width, 40 inches.
With blue and gold brocade mounting, 105 and 47 inches, respectively.

A typical Chinese landscape, with pavilions, lake and mountain scenery, rendered with subtle lines and in soft colors on brown-toned silk. The details, with habitations scattered here and there, include boatmen, figures and pine trees. Ascribable to a master of the later XIIIth or early XIVth century.

517—LARGE LANDSCAPE

Height of painting, 68½ inches; width, 49½ inches.
With gold brocade mounting, 100 inches and 56½ inches.

Presenting a scholar's mountain retreat, including a lake with boats. The foreground shows a winding stream spanned by bridge, on which is a horseman. Tall pine trees, picturesque rocks and mountain peaks are in the distance. This painting, on brown silk, showing the softness of old tapestry, bears an inscription, the seal of the former owner, and the name of the artist. Ming Dynasty.

518—LANDSCAPE WITH ARCHITECTURE

Painting: Height, 71 inches; width, 37 inches.
With gold brocade mounting, 111 inches and 44 inches, respectively.

Rendered in soft colors, on light brownish-toned silk, representing a scholar's or mandarin's summer home, with busy attendants and approaching visitors. A pavilion is partly visible beyond the trees, while the distance is enclosed by hills. Accessories include terraces and a stream spanned by a bridge. Ming Dynasty.

519—BIRDS AND FLOWERS

Height of painting, 74 inches; width, 54 inches.
With gold brocade mounting, 120 inches and 72 inches.

The painting in softened colors, on brown-toned silk, presenting "one hundred" birds midst flowering trees and bamboo. The feathered gathering includes peacocks, pheasants, cranes, egrets, martins, magpies, ducks, swallows and many other birds that pay tribute to the fabled *fêng-huang*. Naturally rendered and showing harmonious coloring, with technical force and fine composition. Attributed to the Ming Dynasty. (Either by Lu Ki or Liang Chi.)

520—LANDSCAPE AND FIGURE PANEL

Height, 25 inches; width, 38 inches.
With silk brocade mounting, 104 inches and 45 inches, respectively.

The composition with a pavilion inhabited by a scholar, who is about to receive a visitor appearing on horseback and attended by servants and banner-men; probably an historical episode, or connected with a romance of feudal times. Accessories in vigorous line rendering, including pine trees, picturesque rocks, a rapidly flowing stream, and flowering shrubs in the foreground. The distance depicts green hills. The painting bears a long inscription. Ming Dynasty.

521—CHINESE MONOCHROME PAINTING IN INDIA INK

Height, 75 inches; width, 49 inches.
With brocade mounted framing, 120 inches and 68 inches.

Representing a large storm dragon, vigorously rendered midst cloud forms, on tan-colored silk. This creature is conceived as the genius of water and mist, producing storms and rain. It is rendered with great force and bold strokes. Signed by the artist, with his seal. Ming Dynasty.

522—GROUP OF HORSES, PAINTED ON SILK, WITH MOUNTING

Height, 49½ inches; width, 25½ inches.
With gold brocade mounting, 87 inches and 31 inches, respectively.

Five steeds of differing breeds are pictured roaming freely in a field, close to a clump of trees. Bears former owner's seal marks. By Ch'ao Meng-fu(?).

523—MOUNTAINOUS LANDSCAPE WITH FIGURES

Painting: Height, 79 inches; width, 42 inches.
With gold brocade mounting, 105 inches and 50 inches, respectively.

The painting in soft colors on brown-toned silk presenting a picturesque landscape with lofty hills and mountains, intersected by a stream with a bridge. A pavilion is depicted above, occupied by three scholars, within sound of a cascade, the foreground showing travelers on foot and a mounted official on the bridge. Bears seal. Ascribed to the artist Tai Wen Chin, early XVth century.

524—LANDSCAPE WITH CRANES ON BROWNISH-TONED SILK

Height, 7 feet; width. 6 feet.
With the brocaded mounting, 11 feet and 6 feet 8 inches, respectively.

The painting presents a pair of white Manchurian cranes, characterized by the bare crimson poll, crossing on an old pine tree that has fallen athwart a swirling stream, close to which appear bamboo shoots. The composition symbolizes longevity, and the rendering is masterly. These birds are supposed to become superior to the necessity of other sustenance than water, after completing an age of six hundred years. Attributable to the Sung Dynasty (Muh Ki, or Ma Yüan). Late XIIth or early XIIIth century.

(*Illustrated.*)

525—FAN PANEL WITH GLASS MOUNTING

Height, 18½ inches; width, 21¾ inches.

Obverse, painted by the late Dowager Empress, presenting a delicately rendered pink peony flower with stems and leafage, inscribed and bearing the Imperial seal. The reverse discloses the writing of an old tutor who was at the Imperial palace for three generations.

526—SPLIT-BAMBOO BIRD-CAGE

Height, 18½ inches; diameter, 13½ inches.

Large rounded form, with dark staining, including cloisonné and carved ivory mounting. Crowned by a hook of gilt bronze, including cloisonné enamel details. Complete interior equipment including ivory cross bars, or perches, utensils and cloisonné enameled cups. Base has ivory inlaying. Date: XVIIIth century.

527—CHINESE BIRD-CAGE

Height, 23 inches; diameter, 14 inches.

Large rounded form, finished in black lacquer, with rich mountings of carved ivory, bronze crowning and dragon-shaped hook. Complete with interior utensils, partly in ivory and porcelain. Date: XVIIIth century.

528—PEARL INLAID BLACK LACQUER PALACE TABLE

Height, 32½ inches; length, 64 inches; depth, 26 inches.

Oblong shape with square legs; the lacquer finish enriched by pearl inlaying in flower, scroll and fret designs. The top sustaining a large peony flower and pheasant design, enclosed by a diaper and floral vignetted bordering.

529—TWO TEAKWOOD ARMCHAIRS

In Chinese design with plain wood seats, and arms and backs containing panels carved with dragon motifs.

530—LOW TEAKWOOD TABLE

Height, 14 inches; length, 52½ inches; depth, 15 inches.

Of oblong form, in conventional Chinese design, with openwork borders on front and ends. The top, between upturned ends, is made of an inserted panel or gnarled grape-wood that shows an interesting grain and brown color. Has four drawers lined with brown lacquer.

531—CARVED TEAKWOOD PALACE TABLE

Height, 34 inches; length, 58 inches; depth, 25½ inches.

Oblong shape, with inset panels of carved cinnabar lacquer on all sides, representing Imperial five-clawed dragons amid cloud forms. The teakwood top is bordered with silver wire inlaying in floral, diaper and fret patterns.

534

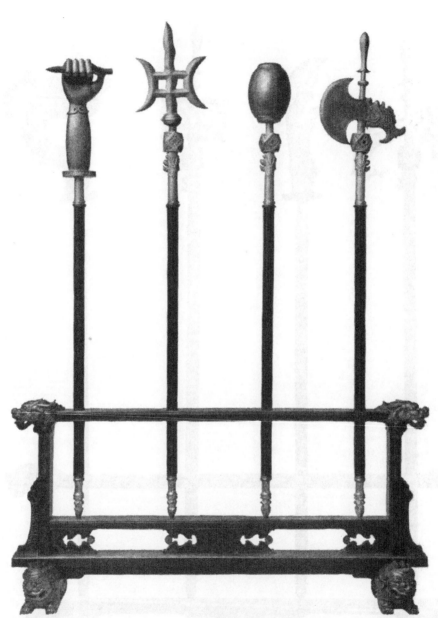

535

532—CARVED TEAKWOOD PALACE TABLE

Height, 34 inches; length, 58 inches; depth, 25½ inches.

Matching the preceding. With similar carved red lacquer panels and silver wire inlay in top.

533—LARGE CHINESE COROMANDEL LACQUER SCREEN

Height, 9 feet; width of each panel, 19 inches; total length, 19 feet.

Consisting of twelve panels or folds, with incised and colored details on a black ground that has turned brown from age; executed during the period of Emperor K'ang-hsi. A ceremonial palace subject (*Kung-shih*) is presented, with occupations of ladies of the court (in the style of Kiu-ying, a Ming artist), showing characteristic architecture and dress of a remote and luxurious dynasty; probably inspired by the *Han King Ch'un* (springtime in the palace of the Han), attributed to the above-named artist.

The panoramic composition, with pavilions, gardens, bridges and trees, is centered by an elevated "dragon pavilion" (*lung-ting*), where the Empress appears entertaining a princess who is interested in watching the court dancers. The scene includes numerous groups of ladies engaged in a succession of pastimes, games or elegant accomplishments. Some appear on the water in a picturesque "phœnix barge," while others in the vast pleasaunce ride ponies or approach the guarded entrance to the inner precincts, with insignia. Still others watch over groups of children and their games, or serve refreshments.

The wide upper border is filled with varied Mandarin objects, baskets of flowers and symbolic fruits. The bordering at either end presents a *Ch'u-shou* motif, which includes dragons and varied animals known to Chinese mythical zoology, and this is continued on the wide lower border. The reverse is decorated with another wide border showing symbolical flowers, fruit, art objects and sacred relics or emblems of the Taoist and Buddhist cults. The screen bears long inscriptions of praise and congratulations for the recipient on a seventieth birthday anniversary, with seals and the date, in the reign of K'ang-hsi. Ta Ch'ing Dynasty.

534—FOUR CEREMONIAL HALBERDS WITH STAND

Width, 6 feet; height, including spears, 6 feet 7 inches.

Ornamental procession halberds and spears (*kang cha*), the varied pewter head-pieces, or insignia of rank, mounted on red lacquer shafts of wood. Open red lacquer stand, of narrow oblong form, carved with dragon heads and supported upon two red lacquered lions.

(Illustrated.)

535—ANOTHER STAND OF FOUR HALBERDS

Including Imperial and scholarly insignia of rank, in pewter, and matching preceding. Mounted with red lacquer shafts of wood. Used for procession and ceremonial purposes. Size similar to preceding.

(*Illustrated.*)

536—LARGE ANTIQUE CHINESE RUG

12 feet 10 inches by 15 feet 7 inches.

Fine close pile; field of diapered old ivory tones with large center medallion, enclosing conventional lotus flowers in varied tones of yellow, soft red and blue shadings. Woven with four borders of varied detail and coloring, which agreeably harmonize with both medallion and field. Ta Ming Dynasty.

AMERICAN ART ASSOCIATION,
MANAGERS.

THOMAS E. KIRBY,
AUCTIONEER.